By the Editors of Consumer Guide®

CARS OF THE 60s

Published by:
Beekman House
A Division of Crown Publishers, Inc.
One Park Avenue
New York, N.Y. 10016

Library of Congress Catalog Card Number: 79-90105
ISBN: 0-517-301857

Cover Photo Credits: R.M. Langworth, Neil Perry, Buick Div. General Motors, Ford Motor Company, Oldsmobile Div. General Motors.

Automobiles of the 1960s

1968 Chrysler Newport Convertible

1968 AMC Javelin SST

1965 Ford Mustang

1961 Chevrolet Corvette

The decade of the '60s was not that long ago. Headlines from that turbulent era are still fresh in our memory. And it's not at all difficult to remember the cars: the 18-foot-long luxury hardtops, the bucket-seat sporty compacts, the personal cars, the ponycars, and the muscle cars of 1960-1969. An incredible assortment of types represented the domestic auto industry in those years. There was one for every taste and budget, from the $1,700 Metropolitan to the $18,500 Crown Imperial limousine. The slogans with which those cars were promoted are also memorable. Who can forget the Wide-Tracks, Scat Packs, SC/Ramblers, Road Runners, Super Stockers, and Youngmobiles? Truly, the '60s were, as Ford put it, the decade of "Total Performance." Cheap petroleum and unprecedented technology combined to bring us cars the likes of which we shall never see again.

As the United States emerged from World War II, few people imagined that such cars would ever be produced. Prophets could not have foreseen multi-passenger production automobiles that could reach 60 miles an hour in 4.6 seconds, or 170 mph on the Bonneville Salt Flats. Yet the Pontiac GTO and the Studebaker Avanti, respectively, did just that.

We're all very practical now. Legitimate concern about the quality of the air we breathe and the high incidence of traffic accidents has led to government intervention in the American automobile industry. As early as 1963, it was decreed that all American cars would have amber parking lights. Soon the list of required features included seat belts, illuminated dashboard controls, running lights, and headrests.

Government demands that the car makers clean up exhaust emissions and make their cars safer were good ideas, even if the legislation that followed was often controversial. But these mandates also guaranteed an end to the uninhibited automotive experimentation of the 1960s.

In a way, the public had as much to do with the decline of innovation in the late '60s as the government did. What incentive was there for the car makers to develop a really innovative model when car buyers seemed interested mainly in performance, styling, and gadgetry? Consider the record. After high initial interest in the Corvair, people soon forgot it existed—long before Ralph Nader's book was published. Buyers yawned at the first Pontiac Tempests, shrugged when informed of their independent rear suspension and rear-mounted transaxle. Tempests sold well, but might have done that well or better with a conventional drive train. Oldsmobile introduced a radical, superbly engineered front-wheel-drive car, the 1966 Toronado, and it was regularly outsold by the conventional Buick Riviera. Pontiac's overhead-cam six of 1966, an engine that offered a better combination of economy and performance than any other six on the market, was almost completely ignored as many customers insisted on big-block V-8s.

Sales records aside, there is something significant about the technological tours de force of the '60s. Nearly all of them came from General Motors. There are many reasons for this. The decline of the independents after World War II and the subsequent mergers and disappearance of Nash, Hudson, Kaiser, Willys, Packard, and Studebaker radically altered the nature of the industry. High-volume manufacturers were soon faced not with one or two markets, but six or eight. They had to meet the need for every kind of automobile: compact, sporty-compact, intermediate, standard, luxury, and personal-specialty. There was no longer any precise distinction of price or purpose among makes. Between 1955 and 1970, the automotive market subdivided. Chevrolet, for example, wasn't building more cars in 1970 than it had built in 1960, but it was building a far greater variety of cars.

General Motors was best able to adapt to the new situation. Ford had successes—like the Mustang, the Continental Mark III, and the Torino—but they were successes of packaging or marketing, not of technology. General Motors was so big that it could just as easily produce radical cars like the Corvair or Toronado as it could conventional cars like the Impala.

Despite the domination of the market by GM and Ford, a few specialty manufacturers operated profitably during the '60s by filling small but significant market needs that had been overlooked by the large companies. The Avanti II has continued to fill one such need up to the present day, long after its company of origin fell apart. The Shelby GT-350 was built around a Mustang by a former racer who believed there was a market for all-out performance. Checker sold 6,000 cars a year to those who wanted to own a taxicab-tough automobile. Brooks Stevens found that others shared his dream of a "modern classic" and would buy an Excalibur.

The buying public did not always react enthusiastically to the introduction of important automotive engineering advances in the 1960s, but buyers did become more sophisticated in their judgment of some gimmicky or useless features. Almost immediately as the decade began, American car buyers started to reject such things as tail fins, push-button automatic transmissions, retractable hardtops, and chrome-bedecked super-cruisers. Rapidly, new models from makes such as Pontiac, Lincoln, Dodge, and Chevrolet illustrated that good design meant more than a five-pound hood ornament. The early compacts showed us that practical cars could be built again, after a generation of impractical ones. The sporty compacts brought home a point that Europeans had long accepted: One should not buy the *biggest* car one can afford, but the *best* car one can afford. We learned a lot in the '60s.

Buying a Car of the '60s

Today, these cars are rapidly replacing models from the '50s as the hottest area of growth among the quarter million car collectors. Aside from technical or design merits, such cars make perfect sense for everyday transportation. Unencumbered by emission controls, many of these '60s cars deliver better gas mileage than more recent cars of comparable size, weight, and engine type. Good ones with low mileage generally cost less than similar new models. And a growing number of 1960s cars are good investments, providing a hedge against inflation more rewarding than a savings account and safer than the stock market. One of the purposes of this book is to review some of the 1960-1969 automobiles that are worthy of becoming, or have already become, collectors' items.

Where do you find one if you want to buy one? The first place to look is your local newspaper. An owner who has had a car since it was new might be more concerned with finding a good home for the old beast than with making a lot of money. The next place to check is the back row of used-car lots, especially in the West and Southwest where rust is not a big problem. Millions of '60s automobiles are still on the road, and are traded in every day. Occasionally, you can take one off a lot for a "book value," which is far lower than collector value.

For the widest variety of choice, it's helpful to subscribe to one of the old-car publications which contain large classified-ad sections. These periodicals also contain a great deal of information about cars, parts, literature, and services. They are:

Hemmings Motor News, P.O. Box 380, Bennington, VT 05201. (A monthly, circulation 175,000.)
Old Cars newspaper, Krause Publications, Iola, WI 54945. (Weekly, 100,000.)
Cars & Parts, P.O. Box 482, Sidney, OH 45367. (Monthly, 75,000.)

Prices in the collector periodicals generally tend to be higher than those in newspapers, especially for "hot" items like Corvettes and Shelby Mustangs. It pays to do a lot of comparison shopping and pricing before taking a plunge. It also pays to spend more for a car in excellent condition than to spend a small amount for one in need of restoration. You'll end up spending less in the long run.

We have isolated three categories of 1960-69 cars that are worthy of consideration. We believe that, 10 or 20 years from now, every car in each list will be acknowledged as a "classic of the '60s."

Blue Chip Collectables. These are the hot ones, already recognized and sought-after by collectors. Prices are high and getting higher, though a few bargains might still exist.

Automobiles of the 1960s

1968-69 American Motors AMX
1965-69 Avanti II
1963-65 Buick Riviera
1960 Cadillac Eldorado Brougham
1968-69 Chevrolet Camaro Z/28
1965-66 Chevrolet Corvair Corsa
1962-64 Chevrolet Corvair Monza Spyder
1963-67 Chevrolet Corvette Sting Ray
1960-62 Chrysler 300F-300H
1969 Dodge Charger Daytona
1960 Edsel Ranger convertible
1965-69 Excalibur SSK roadster
1965-69 Ford Mustang V-8 convertible/fastback
1962-63 Ford Thunderbird Sports Roadster
1965-66 Imperial
1961-67 Lincoln Continental convertible
1967-69 Mercury Cougar XR7, GT, GTE
1966-67 Oldsmobile Toronado
1967-69 Pontiac Firebird 400
1964-66 Pontiac Tempest GTO
1965-66 Shelby GT-350
1963-64 Studebaker Avanti
1962-64 Studebaker Gran Turismo Hawk

Secondary Collectibles and "Comers." The following cars are likely to appreciate rapidly in value. Their potential may lie in low original production, innovative engineering, interesting styling, and/or very high performance.

1968-69 American Motors Javelin SST
1966-67 American Motors Marlin
1966-67 Buick Riviera
1962 Buick Wildcat
1960-69 Cadillac Eldorado
1963-67 Checker Town Limousine
1967-69 Chevrolet Camaro
1960 Chevrolet Corvair Monza
1960-62 Chevrolet Corvette
1968-69 Chevrolet Corvette
1965-67 Chevrolet Impala SS
1963-65 Chrysler 300J-300L
1960 Chrysler Saratoga
1966-68 Chrysler Sportsgrain convertible
1968-69 Continental Mark III
1960 Continental Mark V formal limousine
1960 DeSoto Adventurer hardtop
1961 DeSoto
1964-69 Dodge Hemi V-8 models
1966-67 Dodge Charger
1968-69 Dodge Charger R/T
1967-69 Dodge Coronet R/T & Super Bee
1960 Edsel
1965-69 Excalibur phaeton/roadster
1965-68 Ford Mustang 6
1960-63 Ford Thunderbird
1967-68 Imperial convertible

1961-67 Lincoln Continental sedan
1967-68 Mercury Brougham
1964-69 Mercury Comet Cyclone
1969 Mercury Marauder X-100
1967-68 Mercury Marquis
1962-63 Oldsmobile F-85 Jetfire
1964-65 Oldsmobile Jetstar I
1961-64 Oldsmobile Starfire
1965-69 Plymouth Barracuda fastback
1965-68 Plymouth Belvedere SS/Hemi/GTX
1968-69 Plymouth Road Runner
1967-69 Pontiac Firebird
1967-69 Pontiac GTO
1962-69 Pontiac Grand Prix
1965 Rambler Marlin
1967-69 Shelby
1963-64 Studebaker Lark Daytona
1963-64 Studebaker Wagonaire V-8

Everyday Alternatives. As new-car prices continue to rise, the economical compacts and intermediates of the '60s make increasing sense to people who have the instincts of a collector. Parts for most of them are still readily available.

1966-69 American Motors Ambassador 6
1968-69 American Motors Javelin 6
1968 American Motors Rebel convertible
1961-62 Buick Special Skylark
1967-69 Chevrolet Camaro 6
1961-62 Chevrolet Corvair Lakewood wagon
1961-69 Chevrolet Corvair Monza
1963-69 Dodge Dart GT
1961-62 Dodge Lancer GT
1961-63 Ford Falcon Futura/Sprint
1962-63 Mercury Comet S-22
1967-68 Mercury Cougar
1961-62 Metropolitan
1962-63 Oldsmobile F-85
1965-69 Plymouth Barracuda
1966-67 Plymouth Belvedere
1961-64 Plymouth Valiant Signet
1967-69 Pontiac Firebird ohc 6
1961-63 Pontiac Tempest
1966-67 Pontiac Tempest ohc 6
1964-69 Rambler American/Rogue
1965 Rambler Ambassador 6
1967 Rambler Rebel
1960-64 Studebaker Lark convertible/hardtop
1965-66 Studebaker

Note to the reader: In charts accompanying each chapter, horsepower figures are for gross hp, not net.

PHOTO CREDITS: American Motors Corp.; Avanti Motors Corp.; Checker Motors Corp.; Chrysler Corp.; Excalibur Automotive Corp.; Ford Motor Co.; General Motors Corp.; Richard M. Langworth; Studebaker photos from the Applegate and Applegate Collection.

AMC
American Motors Corp.
Kenosha, Wisconsin

AMC began registering some of its cars as individual makes in 1966-67, when the "Rambler" prefix for the Ambassador and Marlin was dropped. In 1968 the Rebel, AMX, and Javelin were added. All these AMC marques are covered here. (The Rambler story appears later in this book.)

The top-of-the-line 1966 Ambassador was a close copy of the completely redesigned 1965 Rambler Ambassador. The '66 was perhaps one of the best designs to come from the studios of Richard A. Teague, AMC's vice-president of styling. It rode a 116-inch wheelbase—four inches longer than that of the '64 version—and was a graceful-looking car. A new model for 1966 was the elegantly appointed DPL hardtop, which was equipped with reclining bucket seats, fold-down center armrests, plush pile carpeting,

and an extensive list of accessories. Ranked below the DPL was a series of Ambassador sedans, station wagons, hardtops, and a convertible in the basic 880 and luxury 990 models. Ambassadors were available with the long-running "Typhoon" 232 cubic-inch six, which developed 155 horsepower, or with two V-8 engines—a 287 cubic-inch power plant with 198 hp, and a 327 cubic-inch engine with 250 or 270 hp. The 270-hp power plant had a 9.7:1 compression ratio and required premium gasoline; all other AMC engines ran on regular. Although most Ambassadors were ordered with automatic transmission, a few were equipped with a three-speed manual transmission or "Twin-Stick" overdrive. A four-speed synchromesh floor shift was also marketed for the 990 and DPL models.

The big Ambassadors evolved nicely through the

1966 Ambassador DPL Two-Door Hardtop

1967 Ambassador DPL Two-Door Hardtop

1966 Ambassador 990 Convertible

1967 Marlin

1966 Ambassador 990 Cross-Country Station Wagon

1967 Marlin

AMC

late 1960s. For 1967, their wheelbases were lengthened and their fastback styling was modified. The following year the hood was refined and a new model sequence appeared with three series: basic, DPL, and SST. New front styling, which included a sculptured hood, plastic grille, and horizontal instead of vertical headlights, arrived in 1969. By '69, the Ambassador wheelbase had grown to 122 inches, and air conditioning was standard equipment.

A radical and unsuccessful attempt was made on the personal car market with the Rambler Marlin of 1965, and subsequent 1966-67 AMC Marlin. Styled by Teague, the Marlin was a huge fastback with rakish rear side windows. The '66 was changed from 1965 only by a new grille, a sway bar for six-cylinder models, and an optional black vinyl-covered roof. The 1967 Marlin was the last of the line. It was built on a 118-inch

wheelbase, and was 6.5 inches longer than the previous models. This was perhaps the nicest-looking Marlin of all three years. But the car's styling was not popular, and Marlin production was never high: Fewer than 4,600 were built for 1966, and only 2,545 for 1967. They'd offered some of the accoutrements of a sports car—optional four-speed transmission, tachometer, bucket seats, engines ranging up to the 343 cubic-inch V-8 with 280 hp—but not a sports car's taut, precise handling.

A more successful model was the 1968 AMC Javelin, a ponycar in the Mustang image, beautifully shaped and exciting. More than 56,000 Javelins were built that year, and this helped American Motors recover from a four-year sales slump. With the standard 232 six, the Javelin could cruise at 80 miles an hour; with the optional 290 cid V-8, it could cruise at 100 mph; with the ultra-high-performance "Go Package" (343 V-8 with four-barrel carburetor, dual exhausts, power disc brakes, heavy-duty suspension and wide tires), it would run from 0 to 60 in eight seconds

1968 Rebel SST Two-Door Hardtop

1968 AMX

1969 Ambassador SST Four-Door Sedan

1968 Rebel SST Convertible

1968 Javelin

1968 Rebel SST Convertible

and approach 120 mph. It was roomier, larger, and longer than its rivals—Mustang, Camaro, and Barracuda. It was also a cleaner design. Javelin had few changes (twin venturi grille, new wheel covers, revised body striping) for the 1969 model year, when production totaled 40,675 units.

An exciting mid-1968 introduction was the AMX, a two-seat Javelin with a 97-inch wheelbase. AMX introduced the new AMC 390-cid V-8. This big mill developed 315 hp and 425 foot-pounds of torque. Its design included a crankshaft and connecting rods of forged steel. The standard AMX engine was a 290 cubic-inch V-8 with 225 hp; a 343 with 280 hp was available as an option. The car's tight suspension, comprehensive instrumentation, bucket seats, and optional four-speed gearbox made the AMX a genuine sports car, and it did well in competition.

AMX production was 6,725 units for model year 1968, and 8,293 for 1969. This was a disappointment for AMC's management, which had hoped to attain the 20,000-unit mark. After 1970, when 4,116 models were built, the series was phased out. (However, the AMX name was used from time to time on sporty American Motors cars during the 1970s.)

Another new AMC make was the '68 Rebel, which had been a model of the Rambler through 1967. Rebel was AMC's intermediate, having a 114-inch wheelbase, a variety of six-cylinder and V-8 engines, and a competitive price structure starting around $2,500. Sedans, hardtops, station wagons, and convertibles were offered in three series: the 550, 770, and SST. Rebels were the only AMC cars available with soft tops in 1968, but such models were rare: only 377 convertibles in the 550 series and 823 in the SST version were produced. These were the last of the AMC convertibles. Rebels for 1969 were offered only in basic and SST form. They had a wide track and new grille, deck, and taillights.

American Motors' new makes during the late '60s were a diverse lot. Some of them, like the AMX and Javelin, were top-flight automobiles. But the company's attempt to meet Big Three competition in every

1969 Ambassador SST Four-Door Sedan

1969 Rebel SST Two-Door Hardtop

1969 Javelin

market sector ultimately condemned it to also-ran status. And the market Rambler carved out in the early 1960s had been infiltrated by the Big Three already. Ironically, the Rambler proved too successful for its own good. It had shown the industry giants a whole new market, much to AMC's misfortune.

AMERICAN MOTORS AT A GLANCE, 1960-1969										
	1960	1961	1962	1963	1964	1965	1966	1967	1968	1969
Price Range, $							2404-2968	2619-3143	2443-3207	2484-3998
Weight Range lbs.							2970-3180	3279-3486	2826-3475	2826-3732
Wheelbases, in.							116	118	97-118	97-122
6 Cyl. Engines, hp							145-155	155	145-155	145-155
8 Cyl. Engines, hp							198-270	200	200-315	200-315

Avanti II

Avanti Motor Corp.
South Bend, Indiana

When Studebaker left the car business in 1964, Leo Newman and the late Nathan Altman had been partners in one of the oldest Studebaker dealerships in the country. Two years later, Newman and Altman resurrected the Avanti, Studebaker's greatest car of the '60s.

The Studebaker Avanti, designed by a team of Raymond Loewy stylists, had been a failure in the marketplace, but it was loved by hardcore Studebaker enthusiasts. It was the only Studebaker in two generations to have inspired such interest. It held every major U. S. Auto Club record, including a 170.78-mph flying mile at Bonneville. Newman and Altman decided the Avanti was too good to lose, so they bought the rights to its name and manufacture, and a portion of Studebaker's abandoned car factory in South Bend. Avanti II production commenced in late 1965. The goal was an output of 300 cars a year. That figure was never achieved, but production was adequate and consistent.

Unlike its forebear, the Avanti II was a business success. Fiberglass body panels insured that there would be no expensive sheet metal dies to maintain; hand construction on a miniature assembly line meant that each car could be built carefully and tailored to each customer's specifications. Altman, a born salesman, reveled in the Avanti II business. Visitors to the factory would see him with telephone in hand, helping an affluent customer to individualize a car long-distance.

The Avanti II is still in production, and its base price of about $18,000 makes it a fair bargain. In the 1960s, though, it was an even better buy: Prices began at $6,550! Even the most dedicated devotee of high living was hard put to push the price of a tailor-made model up to $10,000, though Newman and Altman tried their best to help. The option list included a Hurst four-speed shifter, power steering, air conditioning, electric window lifts, tinted windshield and rear window, AM/FM radio, Eppe fog or driving lights, limited-slip differential, Magnum 500 chromed wheels, and a variety of Firestone and Michelin bias-ply and radial tires. The basic Avanti II came with vinyl trim, but textured "Raphael vinyl" could be ordered for $200 extra. Genuine leather seats and door panel trim cost $300, and leather trim throughout went for $500. Any color paint would be used to suit any preference.

Although early Avanti IIs used the same modified Studebaker convertible frame as the original Avanti, they did not use Studebaker V-8 engines. (The supply

Avanti II

Avanti II

of those power plants dried up when Studebaker left South Bend). Instead, the manufacturers used the Chevrolet Corvette Sting Ray V-8, which at first displaced 327 cubic inches, and was later enlarged to 350 cid. Buyers could choose a fully synchronized Borg-Warner four-speed manual transmission, or Avanti's power-shift automatic, which was designed to permit manual shifting in first and second. All these mechanical changes were hidden from view, under a body that was identical with that of the original Avanti. The only clue that a new model was something other than an original was its level stance (Altman's customers disliked the original's front-end rake), and the addition of a Roman numeral II to the Avanti script.

The Corvette engine provided excellent performance for the aerodynamic four-place grand tourer. A typical 0 to 60 acceleration time for an Avanti II with automatic was under nine seconds; with a 3.54:1 rear axle ratio, the car could achieve 125 miles per hour. The Chevy V-8 was lighter than the old Studebaker engine, so it improved Avanti's front-rear weight distribution from the 59-41 of the original car to 57-43. The new car understeered, but final oversteer could be induced by a judicious poke at the throttle. The front disc and rear drum brakes resisted fade and provided nearly 1G deceleration from an 80-mph panic stop. Obviously, Newman and Altman cared about safety, as well as straight-line performance.

The Avanti II sold to a clientele somewhat different from that of the Studebaker version. In the 1960s, $6,500 was Cadillac Eldorado money; the original Avanti had sold for $4,445, in Chrysler territory. Newman and Altman realized that this difference in price meant a change in market appeal. Accordingly, their promotion was aimed at the "personal luxury" customer rather than the performance buyer.

On the open road, the Avanti II was in its element. Road testers gave the car points for safety, low noise level, rigidity of structure, and a firm but comfortable ride. "In this day of great concern over automotive safety," wrote John R. Bond, "the Avanti II should make new friends, for obviously there was more thought given to safety in its conception than in most American cars. Good brakes, sensible interior design and decent handling impart security to the driver . . . It's a better car than it was three years ago."

Every Avanti II ever made is a collector's item. Good ones rarely can be found anymore for less than $10,000. Enthusiasts hope they'll continue building them forever.

AVANTI II AT A GLANCE, 1960-1969										
	1960	1961	1962	1963	1964	1965	1966	1967	1968	1969
Price Range, $						NA	7200	5795-7200	6645	7145
Weight, lbs.						3217	3181	3217	3217	3217
Wheelbases, in.						109	109	109	109	109
8 Cyl. Engines, hp						300	300	300	300	300

Buick

Buick Motor Division of General Motors Corp.
Flint, Michigan

For Buick, the 1960s were very successful years. The division built about 300,000 cars in 1960, and thus ranked ninth in the industry. During 1969 Buick built more than 713,000 cars, and moved up to fourth place. The improvement was in part due to the debut of the Special and Skylark, Buick's new compacts, and in part the result of increases in production of large Buick models. For example, some 56,000 Electras were produced in 1960; nearly 159,000 in 1969. LeSabre production was about 152,000 units in 1960, and nearly 198,000 in '69. The Wildcat, a 1963 replacement for the Invicta, began at the 35,000-unit level, but almost doubled that figure by 1969.

The 1961 Buick Special was one of the "second wave" compacts from GM—the Buick-Oldsmobile-Pontiac cars that followed the 1960 Chevrolet Corvair. The Special's first engine was a 215 cubic-inch aluminum block V-8 that was light, smooth-running, efficient, and economical. This quiet, powerful engine has had a long life. Today, in modified form, it powers the new Rover 3500 and Land Rover V-8 sold by Jaguar Rover Triumph (formerly British Leyland).

To profit from the sporty-car market pioneered in 1960 by Chevrolet's Corvair Monza, Buick introduced the mid-1961 Special Deluxe Skylark. This coupe had bucket seats, deluxe trim, vinyl-covered roof, and a 185-horsepower version of the aluminum V-8. More than 12,000 units were sold before the end of the

model year. In 1962, when Buick introduced a Skylark convertible and an optional Borg-Warner four-speed transmission, sales increased to more than 42,000 cars.

During the early '60s the large Buicks were changed dramatically. The 1960 LeSabre, Invicta, Electra, and Electra 225—sedans, station wagons, two-door and four-door hardtops and convertibles—were large, heavy cars of dubious styling. Their 1961 replacements were altered in wheelbase, were 100 to 200 pounds lighter, and had much cleaner lines. In 1962, the Wildcat appeared as a subseries of the Invicta. It was a two-ton, 123-inch-wheelbase luxury hardtop priced at nearly $4,000. Wildcats were equipped with bucket seats, vinyl-covered roof, and special exterior trim. This car was well received, and returned as a separate Buick model for 1963. Fewer than 3,500 Invictas were sold that year. From 1964 on, the Wildcat was Buick's middle-priced full-size car.

Production of the top-of-the-line Electra steadily increased throughout the 1960s. In 1961 Buick offered two Electras—the basic model, and the more luxurious Electra 225. In 1962, however, the base model was dropped, and all Electras were "225s"; the division then concentrated on fewer models. Electras were powered by Buick's largest engine, the 401 cubic-inch V-8. Horsepower from 1960 to 1963 was 325 at 4400 rpm.

1960 Buick LeSabre Four-Door Sedan

1961 Buick Electra Four-Door Hardtop

1961 Buick Special Four-Door Sedan

1962 Buick Special DeLuxe convertible

1963 Buick Electra 225 Convertible

1963 Buick Riviera

1962 Buick Electra Four-Door Hardtop

1964 Buick Wildcat Two-Door Hardtop

During these years, Buick styling wasn't exceptional. But then the 1963 Riviera, a personal luxury sports coupe, changed the division's image almost overnight. Many people felt that William L. Mitchell, chief of GM styling, had created for the Riviera one of the best automotive shapes of all time.

The Riviera's origins can be found in a Mitchell project to revive the LaSalle (Cadillac's low-priced cousin), which had disappeared in 1940. Numerous renderings and clay models had been made—notably, an experimental 1955 convertible with a LaSalle-type grille, designed by Buick stylist Ned Nickles. The car was named LaSalle II. Although it never went into production, the LaSalle II encouraged GM to build a "personal luxury" competitor to Ford's Thunderbird. Ultimately, GM's management drafted Buick to produce such a vehicle. Cadillac didn't have the facilities, Chevrolet was enjoying record sales, and Oldsmobile and Pontiac were occupied with other projects. And, since Buick sales needed a shot in the arm, the project was assigned to the Flint division. The Riviera name was a natural. It dated back to 1949, when it had been used on one of the first "hardtop-convertibles," an important styling innovation.

The Riviera borrowed some design features from various sources: English coachbuilders inspired its razor-shaped body creases, for instance. But the resultant styling was unique. The final clay model was approved by early 1961, and 40,000 Rivieras were scheduled for production in the 1963 model year. Riding a 117-inch wheelbase, they were about 14 inches shorter than other Buicks. The 325-horsepower, 401 cubic-inch V-8 engine was standard in 1963. A 425 cubic-inch power plant, with up to 360 bhp, was a 1964 option. The transmission was two-speed Turbine Drive in 1963; the three-speed Twin-Turbine Hydra-matic

was used from 1964 on.

The Riviera handled well. Its standing-quarter-mile performance was 16 seconds at 85 mph for the standard V-8; 15.5 seconds and 90-plus mph for the 360-hp engine.

In 1964, Buick's smallest cars were restyled and enlarged. Their wheelbases were 115 inches for sedans, 120 inches for station wagons. The cars also received new engines: a 225 cubic-inch V-6 with 155 hp, and a 333 cubic-inch V-8 with 210 hp. The plush Skylark models were considered as part of the Special series, though they are listed individually in our model year production charts. People liked the luxury they offered, and by 1964 Skylarks were rapidly becoming the most popular Buick compact. The production ratio of basic Skylarks to Specials was about 9 to 10 in 1964. Then, from 1965 on, Skylark production pulled away, and by 1969 Buick was building nearly five Skylarks to every one Special.

The large Buicks—LeSabre, Wildcat, and Electra—were lengthened in 1964, although no change was made in wheelbase. The LeSabre's standard engine became a 300 cubic-inch V-8 that developed 325 hp. Wildcats were the hot rods of the family, since they combined the 401 cubic-inch Electra engine with the lighter, shorter LeSabre chassis. As such, the Wildcat played the performance role in the same manner as the Buick Century of the 1950s had. Rivieras, meanwhile, remained basically unchanged for 1964, though a 425-cid engine was added to the option list.

In the first half of the decade, Buick's output rose by 50 percent. The division climbed from ninth to seventh place. And instead of a limited series of large cars that were priced just below Cadillac models, Buick offered large and intermediate-size cars, plus the unique Riviera. The Riviera consistently sold at the rate of

Buick

35,000 to 40,000 units a year. In 1965, Riviera's headlights were hidden behind the grille, and the taillights were integrated with the rear bumper.

The year 1965 was significant in other ways, too. Numerous trim and model variations were offered so the buyer could custom-build his Buick. There were standard, deluxe, and Skylark versions of the Buick Special, with V-6 or V-8 engines, priced from about $2,350 to $3,000; and V-8 Special Sportwagons in the $3,000 to $3,200 range. The Wildcat was offered in standard, deluxe, and custom trim packages as a sedan, hardtop sedan, coupe, and as a deluxe and custom convertible. LeSabres and Electra 225s came in standard and custom versions. The most expensive Buick was the Electra 225 Custom convertible, priced at $4,440. LeSabres were fitted with the 300-cid V-8; Wildcats and Electras with the big 401.

An important Buick performance option in 1965 was the Gran Sport package for the Riviera and Skylark. Gran Sports were equipped with $250 worth of roadability improvements. Equipped with oversize tires, Super Turbine 300 automatic transmission, and the Wildcat 401 engine, which developed 325 hp, the

1965 Buick LeSabre Two-Door Hardtop

1967 Buick Special Four-Door Sedan

1967 Buick Riviera Gran Sport

Skylark Gran Sport was every inch a grand touring car. The Riviera version was, of course, even grander. Using the 360-hp 425-cid engine, it could attain 125 mph on the straight. *Motor Trend* magazine pronounced the Riviera Gran Sport superb in every category: "It goes and handles better than before, and that's quite an improvement."

There were many changes in the Rivieras for 1966-67. Although the crisp, razor-edged design looked much more massive than before, it rode a wheelbase that was only two inches longer than that of the 1965 model. The newer Riviera's smooth sheet metal, its clean, hidden-headlight grille, and large windows melded to create an impressive effect. Yet it sold for only about $4,400, an amount that seems unbelievable today.

Rivieras were the big news from Buick in 1966 because there were relatively few changes in the rest of the division's cars that year. Again in 1967, modest face-lifts of grilles, side trim, and taillights were the biggest alterations. The Riviera received a new grille with a horizontal crossbar and redesigned parking lights. Specials and Skylarks, which continued to offer the 225 V-6 or the 300 V-8, were distinguished by their grilles.

For 1967, Buick introduced one of its largest engines: the 430 cubic-inch V-8, which was standard on the Wildcat, Electra, and Riviera. Its 360 horsepower was no numerical improvement on previous engines (though maximum horsepower had dropped to 340 on the 1966 models), but it ran more smoothly and quietly. Also new was a 400-cid cast-iron V-8 for the Special-Skylark chassis. It developed 340 hp. This power plant appeared in a sporty series with bucket seats, which was called the GS400. A convertible, a hardtop, and a coupe composed the series. An identical hardtop, using the 340 engine, was the GS340. About 15,000 GS-styled Skylarks were sold.

Sales were excellent for Buick in 1967. Calendar-year production came close to 574,000 units, and the division ranked fifth in the industry.

In 1968, the Skylark dominated sales among "small" Buick cars, although it was then considered as an intermediate rather than a compact. A record 178,025 Skylarks were built for the model year. (Only 49,475 Specials were produced.) Buick used three different wheelbases for its junior editions: Special and Skylark two-doors were 112 inches, four-door models and Special Deluxe station wagons were 116 inches, Sportwagons were 121 inches. Again a group of Gran Sport models was fielded. They were the GS350 hardtop, and the GS400 hardtop and convertible. The V-6 engine was increased to a 250 cubic-inch displacement, but its compression was lowered to meet emission requirements, and gross horsepower was 155. The V-8 used was a new 350 cubic-inch power plant that developed 230 hp, or 280 hp on the GS350 model. The 350 V-8 also powered LeSabres, which still retained the wheelbase they'd had in 1960. The 430 V-8 was used for the Wildcat, Electra, and Riviera. Buick's restyling for its 1968 big cars included new

1968 Buick LeSabre Convertible

1969 Buick Sportwagon 400 Station Wagon

1969 Buick Riviera

1969 Buick Electra 225 Two-Door Hardtop

divided grilles, altered rear bumpers, and concealed windshield wipers. Skylarks and Specials were given a downward-sloping side contour line and new grilles. The Riviera received a much heavier, divided grille, and was not quite as clean-looking as it had been in 1966-67. All Buicks other than Rivieras featured a side contour that was reminiscent of the old sweepspear of the 1950s. Since many Buicks also had stylized "ventiports," another trademark, tradition was served.

No engine changes were made for record-breaking 1969, when Buick produced more than 713,000 cars between January and December—its highest output for any calendar year to date—and attained fourth place. The Electra 225, Wildcat, and LeSabre were given new bodies with ventless side windows, new

grilles, and rear treatments. The Riviera received a face-lift, which made its grille look busier. Gran Sports and Sportwagons, meanwhile, were all but separate Buick models now. The lineup of GS350 and GS400 hardtops and convertibles, and Sportwagons with two or three bench seats, was offered as in 1968. LeSabres remained structurally unchanged, but the Wildcat was switched back from the Electra's chassis to the LeSabre's, and was improved in handling.

Buicks of the '60s were remarkably consistent from year to year in design and engineering. The fact that Buick needed no sensational engineering or styling breakthroughs (other than the Riviera) to more than double its production in this decade was a tribute to the sound design and value of its vehicles.

BUICK AT A GLANCE, 1960-1969										
	1960	1961	1962	1963	1964	1965	1966	1967	1968	1969
Price Range, $	2756-4300	2330-4350	2304-4448	2309-4365	2343-4385	2343-4440	2348-4424	2411-4469	2513-4615	2562-4701
Weight Range, lbs.	4139-4653	2579-4441	2638-4471	2661-4340	2983-4362	2977-4344	3009-4323	3071-4336	3125-4314	3126-4328
Wheelbases, in.	123-126.3	112-126	112-126	112-126	115-126	115-126	115-126	115-126	112-126	112-126.2
6 Cyl. Engines, hp			135	135	155	155	160	160	155	155
8 Cyl. Engines, hp	250-325	155-325	155-325	155-325	210-360	210-360	210-340	210-360	230-360	230-360

Cadillac

Cadillac Division of General Motors Corp.
Detroit, Michigan

By the end of the '60s, Cadillac was the undisputed sales leader among American luxury cars. As always, Cadillac emphasized mechanical refinement and the latest comfort and convenience features. But during the '60s, Cadillac styling became much more graceful and restrained than it had been during the previous decade, though still recognizably Cadillac. The more conservative styling approach used in the '60s can be seen in the gradual shrinking of Cadillac's famous tail fins, beginning with the 1960 design. By 1965, the fins (which had reached their greatest height ever on the 1959 Cadillacs) had disappeared into the rear fenders completely.

During the '60s, Cadillac introduced few engineering advances of the sort for which it had become known over the previous 20 years. Instead, the division expanded its model lineup in the '60s and offered the widest selection in the luxury field. The one technically interesting Cadillac of the '60s was the 1967 Eldorado. It was the smallest car that had been built by Cadillac since the LaSalle. Like that earlier car, the Eldorado's

1960 Cadillac Fleetwood 60 Special

1962 Cadillac Series 62 six-window Sedan de Ville

1963 Cadillac four-window Sedan de Ville

handsome styling would influence that of other cars for years to come. It was, and still is, a handsome design. In fact, it was the styling of all Cadillacs in the '60s that helped the division set new sales records almost every year. And in the process of winning more customers, "The Standard of the World" did an artistic about-face. The car that had been the symbol of garish excess in the '50s became the symbol of success and good taste in the '60s.

The Cadillac line was face-lifted for 1960, and the styling of the '60 model was more restrained than the chrome-laden '59 look. The 1960 grille was cleaner and the tail fins were reduced in height. A feature carried over from 1959 was the option of four or six windows on sedan models in the 62 and De Ville series. Both four-window and six-window models cost the same. Prices throughout the line were not changed from the year before. Nor were there any changes in mechanical specifications. The standard horsepower rating was 325; the Eldorado offered 345. Cadillac had dropped to 11th place in production in 1959, but in 1960 it again rose to 10th place. It would continue to hold 10th place—an impressive position for a luxury car—until 1965. Model year 1960 was the last for the limited-edition Eldorado Brougham. Priced at around $13,000, the Brougham sold in very small numbers. Cadillac management had already begun work on a successor that would sell in higher numbers and, therefore, be more profitable.

For 1961, Cadillac styling showed the influence of William L. Mitchell. Mitchell was not terribly fond of chrome and favored a more chiseled look than did Harley Earl, his predecessor as Director of GM Styling. The 1961 models were the first designed by Mitchell's staff and, as a result, were cleaner than any Cadillac had been in years. The grille was reduced in size to a modest grid between the headlights. The wraparound windshield was abandoned (except by the Series 75), yet visibility was improved. The model range shrank in 1961. The Eldorado Seville was dropped, as was the Eldorado Brougham. The only remaining Eldorado was the Biarritz convertible, which used the standard 325-hp engine.

At General Motors, the early 1960s was a period of little styling change. The 1962 Cadillac was no exception. Its tail fins were lowered, cornering lights were added to the front fenders, and air conditioning became standard equipment. Detail trim changes included a slightly flashier grille and a thin bright metal molding positioned low on the body sides. The roofline was squared off on some models. Back-up, turn, and stoplights were combined in a single housing. The rear light lens showed white in daylight and red at night or when the brakes were applied. New models were the 62 Town Sedan and the De Ville Park Avenue, a pair of short-deck, four-door hardtops. The engine remained unchanged from 1961. A new dual braking system, which used separate hydraulic lines for front and rear brakes, was introduced. Cadillac produced over 158,000 cars for calendar year '62, some 10,000 more than the 1961 figure.

Cadillac's V-8 engine was revised in 1963 for the first time in 14 years. Its displacement, bore and stroke, valves, rocker arms, cylinder heads and connecting rods were the same as before. But everything else was different. The new block was stiffer but 50 pounds lighter than its predecessor. Accessory mounting points were redesigned for easier accessibility. The new engine did little to improve Cadillac's already peppy acceleration; but the new power plant was smoother and quieter, in keeping with Cadillac's luxury role. The 1963 models could reach 115 to 120 mph, run 0 to 60 mph in 10 seconds, and accelerate to 80 mph from standstill in 16 seconds. Gas mileage was about 14 miles per gallon. Most impressive was the quietness of these cars at high speed. Many testers thought they were better than the Rolls-Royce in this respect.

The 1963 restyle was something of a departure from recent face-lifts. The fins were still there, but lower than ever. A more massive full-width grille contained parking lights built into grille extensions under the headlamps. New body panels and side moldings created a more slab-sided effect than in past models. The rear end was also more massive-looking, with elongated vertical taillight and back-up light housings.

Prices rose only slightly in 1963, and Cadillacs remained excellent buys. Standard equipment included Hydra-Matic, power steering, power brakes, air conditioning, back-up lights, and remote-control outside mirror. A six-way power seat was standard on the Eldorado. Power windows were standard on all models except Series 62 sedans and coupes. Power vent windows were offered as an option. The specifications included self-adjusting brakes, cornering lights, and directional signal repeaters atop the front fenders. Remarkably, a Series 62 model sold for as little as $5,026 in 1963. Even the Eldorado Biarritz cost only $6,608. Cadillac production topped 164,000 for the calendar year.

Revisions were minor again in 1964. New, lower tail fins—the last true fins to appear on a Cadillac—created an unbroken beltline, accentuating the cars' length. A horizontal bar, painted body color, divided the grille to enhance the impression of width, and there were the usual revised taillamp housings. Cadillac's new Comfort-Control heating and air conditioning system maintained a set temperature regardless of outside conditions. This fully automatic system has been on the Cadillac option list ever since. Sales in 1964 fell slightly to 154,000 units, but this total was still good enough to keep Cadillac number 10 in sales.

Cadillac had a resoundingly successful year in 1965, producing close to 200,000 cars. But it was a banner year for the rest of the industry too, so even this record output was good for only 11th place in production. The

1964 Cadillac Series 62 Coupe

1964 Cadillac Fleetwood Series 75 Limousine

Series 62, a name that had been around since 1940, was replaced by the Calais. The De Ville, Eldorado, 60 Special, and 75 continued as before. The last three also carried Fleetwood nameplates; a wreath-and-crest medallion; broad, bright rocker panel and rear quarter moldings; and rectangular-pattern rear "grilles." A Fleetwood Brougham model, featuring a vinyl roof and "Brougham" script on the rear roof pillars, was added to the series.

The major styling change for 1965 was a longer, lower silhouette on the standard 129.5-inch wheelbase, and the disappearance of the tail fins that had been a Cadillac hallmark since 1948. The 60 Special was given its own 133-inch wheelbase, having shared the standard chassis since 1959. Rear styling consisted of a horizontal rear bumper and vertical rear lamp grouping. There was a new flush contour to the top and rear quarter panels. Curved glass side windows were used for the first time. Horsepower was boosted to 340, giving Cadillac the highest power-to-weight ratio in the industry. All models except the 75 featured "dual driving range" Turbo Hydra-Matic, a perimeter-type frame, and "sonically balanced" exhaust system. Prices remained much as they had been in 1961.

In 1966, Cadillac had its first 200,000-car year. For the January-December period, 205,001 cars were assembled. The 1966 styling was a mild face-lift of the 1965, with new front bumpers, a new grille, and integrated vertical taillight housings. The perimeter frame was used on the 75, which was given its first completely new body since 1959. Variable-ratio power steering, which reduced steering effort for parking and low-speed maneuvers, was introduced on all models. Another new option was heated seats. The Fleetwood Brougham moved one step up the size and prestige ladder by adopting the 133-inch chassis of the 60

Cadillac

Special. The Brougham was more luxuriously trimmed than the Special and accordingly sold for about $320 more.

Some important management changes occurred rapidly at Cadillac in 1965-66. Chief engineer Fred Arnold retired in 1965, after a long and rich career with the division. He was succeeded by Carleton A. Rasmussen. The following year, general manager Harold G. Warner retired in favor of Kenneth N. Scott. Scott was replaced six months later by Calvin J. Werner, who remained general manager until 1969. In July of that year, he was relieved by George R. Elges.

The new front-wheel-drive Eldorado of 1967 is the most significant Cadillac of the '60s. Based on the Oldsmobile Toronado, which had appeared the year before, the new Eldorado utilized a front-wheel-drive transaxle. The car's distinctive razor-edge styling would later be seen on other GM cars. The Eldorado's roofline, for example, appeared on the 1973 Chevrolet Monte Carlo. In market orientation, the 1967 "Eldo" was the long-awaited replacement for the 1957-60 Eldorado Brougham. It was the result of six years of careful planning and research.

The Eldorado project began with a 1959 styling exercise code-named XP-727, which underwent sever-

al revisions during 1960-62. By early 1962, it had been decided that front-wheel-drive would be used, and prototypes were developed with that in mind. For a while, Cadillac considered calling the new car a "LaSalle," but the Eldorado name was thought to be more recognizable by the buying public. A clay model, the XP-825, with square-cut lines, was the direct predecessor of the production 1967 Eldorado.

Compared with the way Olds launched the Torona-do, the front-drive Eldorado was introduced in typically low-key Cadillac fashion. Management preferred it that way, and the extra year of lead time allowed Cadillac engineers to make improvements on the Toronado package. The Eldorado rode better than the Toronado, yet it handled just as well. Its front suspension consisted of torsion bars, A-arms, and telescopic shocks. The rear suspension was semi-elliptic leaf springs with four shock absorbers—two horizontal, two vertical. The chassis had a relatively compact 120-inch wheelbase. It featured a self-leveling control and radially vented caliper front disc brakes.

Cadillac, orchestrating the Eldorado's debut with precision, priced the car at $6,247. Eldorado production was targeted for 10 percent of the division's total, or about 20,000 cars. The actual 1967 calendar year production was 20,728 units. Sales held at over 23,000 in 1968, 1969, and 1970. The Eldorado quickly became established as a technological tour de force—the ultimate Cadillac. And unlike the Eldorado

1966 Cadillac Calais Coupe

1967 Cadillac Fleetwood Eldorado

1966 Cadillac Fleetwood Series 75 Sedan

1967 Cadillac Coupe de Ville

1968 Cadillac Fleetwood Eldorado

1969 Cadillac Coupe de Ville

1968 Cadillac de Ville Convertible

1969 Cadillac Fleetwood Eldorado

Brougham before it, it made money from the day it appeared.

The remainder of the 1967 line again consisted of the Calais, De Ville and Fleetwood series. Grille and fenders were given a slight forward rake. New features standard for all models included printed circuit boards for the instrument panel, automatic level control (standard on Fleetwoods), cruise control, and tilt steering wheel. Bolstered by the new Eldorado, Cadillac built 213,161 cars in calendar 1967.

In 1968, the big news again was the engine. This was an all-new V-8, which displaced 472 cubic inches and produced 375 horsepower. It had been designed specifically to meet the federal government's new emission control requirements, which took effect in 1968. The 472 was extensively proven, having run the equivalent of 500,000 miles in laboratory testing. Other mechanical features of note in 1968 were hidden windshield wipers and a host of new safety devices.

Styling changes on the 1968 Eldorado were limited to a new grille, longer hood, altered side marker lights,

and larger taillights. Other models were also given longer hoods, along with a revised grille and a redesigned trunk lid for increased cargo capacity. The new engine did not provide fuel economy equal to the previous power plant, but it was capable of propelling a Coupe de Ville from 0 to 100 mph in 27.8 seconds.

In 1969, Cadillac production again broke into the top 10 producers with a record 266,798 units for the calendar year. With this figure, Cadillac passed both Chrysler and American Motors to achieve ninth place in production. The Eldorado's front end was revised once more. Its headlights were no longer hidden as in the 1967-68 versions. Other Cadillacs bowed with a completely revamped body that featured a squarer roofline. Headlamps were again horizontal instead of vertical. The parking lights wrapped around at the front, the grille was new, and the hood was longer. One change that was to prove unpopular with customers was the elimination of front vent windows. Prices ranged from around $5500 for the Calais to about $11,000 for the 75 limousine.

CADILLAC AT A GLANCE, 1960-1969										
	1960	1961	1962	1963	1964	1965	1966	1967	1968	1969
Price Range, $	4892-13,075	4892-9748	5025-9937	5026-9939	5048-9960	5059-9960	4986-10,521	5040-10,571	5315-10,768	5484-10,979
Weight Range, lbs.	4670-5560	4560-5420	4530-5390	4505-5300	4475-5300	4435-5260	4390-5435	4447-5436	4570-5385	4555-5555
Wheelbases, in.	130-149.8	129.5-149.8	129.5-149.8	129.5-149.8	129.5-149.8	129.5-149.8	129.5-149.8	120.0-149.8	120.0-149.8	120.0-149.8
8 Cyl. Engines, hp	325-345	325	325	325	340	340	340	340	375	375

Checker

Checker Motors Corp.
Kalamazoo, Michigan

Checker, builder of taxicabs and airport limousines, began marketing passenger cars in 1960. The company's practical four-door sedan was called the Superba. It had the same upright, tank-like styling that had become familiar to everyone who'd ever seen a taxi. The company was steadfast: There'd be no change in this utilitarian but unattractive design from year to year, as long as there were customers who wanted to own a car that could provide a taxi's reliability and durability. The design of the Superba dated back to the A8 taxicab of 1956. It's still the basis for the Checker cabs of today.

The engine used in Checkers of this era was of Continental Motor Company design, roughly the same as that used in Kaisers of the late 1940s and 1950s. It displaced 226 cubic inches, with a bore and stroke of 3.31x4.38 inches. The L-head version, having a 7.3:1 compression ratio, produced 80 horsepower at 3100 rpm. There was also an overhead-valve version, with an 8.0:1 compression ratio, that developed 122 hp at 4000 rpm. Despite a notable difference in performance, either engine could be ordered in 1960 for the same price.

The 1960 Checker Superba was available as a four-door sedan and a four-door station wagon, in standard or Special packages. The Special, which came with upgraded interior trim, sold for about $110 more than the standard model. True to its taxicab heritage, the Superba sedan had a pair of jump seats, which allowed it to carry eight adults. The wagon had a fold-down rear seat that could be folded or unfolded by an electronic servo, controlled from the dashboard. This gimmick and the extra bodywork inherent in wagon design made the Checker station wagon cost about $350 more than the sedan. Power steering, air

conditioning, and automatic transmission were offered as options on all models.

For 1961 the Superba Special was renamed the Marathon, and 14-inch wheels were used on sedans instead of 15-inchers to lower the car's profile. The overhead-valve engine became standard on station wagons. Prices did not change. Air conditioning cost $411 extra; power steering, $64. Like Checker cabs, the Superba and Marathon had a full bank of gauges, a spartan but well-padded interior, wide doors, and a spacious rear compartment.

Offerings for 1962 were the same four models. The only change was the return to 15-inch wheels for the sedans. In 1963 the overhead-valve engine was increased to 141 hp at 4000 rpm. Prices rose slightly—about $100 across the board. Optimistically, Checker decided to introduce a $7,500 Town Custom limousine on a 129-inch wheelbase in '62. In addition to a glassed-off driver's compartment, a full range of power options was offered. Production was limited, though, because demand for the expensive limousine was nil.

In 1964, the Superba name was dropped and all Checkers were called Marathons. This was the last year for the old 226 cubic-inch engine. The 1965 models used engines purchased from Chevrolet: a 230 cubic-inch six with 140 hp; a 283 V-8 with 195 hp; and a 327 V-8 with 250 hp. Six-cylinder Marathon sedans listed at $2,793; the wagon sold at $3,140. Town Custom limousines were still made, but only on special order. The optional 283 V-8 cost $110 extra, automatic transmission was priced at $248, and overdrive cost $108.

In 1966, Checker added a deluxe sedan at $3,567 and a limousine at $4,541, thereby temporarily reestablishing its four-model lineup. But these two cars

1966 Checker Marathon V-8 Four-Door Sedan

1968 Checker Marathon Station Wagon

Checker Taxi

1967 Checker Marathon V-8 Four-Door Sedan

were dropped again for 1967. The deluxe sedan was revived for 1968, and the deluxe limousine reappeared for 1969.

Checkers became faster cars during these years. The Chevy 283 V-8 engine produced 250 hp in 1967. In 1968, the smaller V-8 engine displaced 307 cubic inches and developed 200 hp. The 327 V-8 produced 275 hp. Prices for optional engines in 1968 were low: $108 for the 307; $195 for the 327.

Sales were moderate for Checker in the '60s, although adequate to sustain the production that the firm desired—6,000 to 7,000 units a year. Checker's best year of the decade was 1962, when 8,173 cars were built.

Morris Markin, founder of Checker, never waivered from his goal to build a tough taxicab. If he could sell a few as passenger cars, well and good; but the fickle public, he insisted, would never control the styling or engineering of Checkers. (It isn't widely known, but Nathan Altman had made overtures to Checker as a possible builder of his Avanti II. Markin, however, said the Avanti was too ugly to sell.)

Markin died in 1970. His son David now runs the company.

CHECKER AT A GLANCE, 1960-1969										
	1960	**1961**	**1962**	**1963**	**1964**	**1965**	**1966**	**1967**	**1968**	**1969**
Price Range, $	2542-3004	2542-3004	2642-7500	2642-4200	2814-3160	2793-3140	2874-4541	2874-3075	3221-3913	3290-4969
Weight Range, lbs.	3410-3780	3320-3615	3320-3615	3485-7500	3625-7500	3360-7500	3400-7500	3400-3500	3390-3590	3390-3802
Wheelbases, in.	120	120	120-129	120-129	120	120	120	120	120	120-129
6 Cyl. Engines, hp	80-122	80-122	80-122	80-140	80-140	140	140	140	140	155
8 Cyl. Engines, hp						195-250	250	250	200-275	235-300

Chevrolet

**Chevrolet Division of General Motors Corp.
Detroit, Michigan**

During the 1960s, Chevrolet Division expanded into at least five new areas: compacts with the Corvair and Chevy II, intermediates with the Chevelle, super stockers with the Impala SS, luxury models with the Caprice, and "ponycars" with the Camaro. (The Corvette and Corvair are different enough to be treated separately in this book.) Every new Chevrolet product of the '60s was carefully designed to fill a basic need—and nearly every one succeeded.

Penetration into so many new markets would seem to imply increased production. The division *did* set some records during the decade. But it was only producing some 500,000 more cars at the end of the 1960s than it had been at the beginning, despite the introduction of four additional lines in different size categories. Actually, the market had been subdivided. The departure of independents and the rise of the compact car, followed by the sporty compact and the intermediate, generated more competition for Chevy in the '60s than there had been in the 1950s, despite the smaller number of makes. In many cases, Chevrolet was competing against itself or other GM divisions. Aside from Ford, Chevy had no strong competitor in many fields.

Chevrolet appeared to be offering a wide range of cars by the end of the decade; however, just four wheelbases were used: 108 inches for the Corvair and Camaro, 110 for the Chevy II and Nova, 115 for the Chevelle, and 119 for the big Chevrolets. The only exception was the 1968-69 Chevelle that, with comparable GM compacts like the Buick Special, switched to a 112-inch wheelbase for two-door models and a 116-inch wheelbase for the four-doors.

The big Chevrolets progressed from overstyled outrageousness to clean, crisp elegance during the 1960s. The '60 model was a face-lift of the horrendously finned '59 edition. Those fins were cropped as a result of buyer resistance during 1959; in 1961, the fins were gone. By 1963, an all-new sculptured body erased all traces of the outlandish '50s. Without a change of wheelbase, the large Chevrolets grew bulkier in the last years of the decade. They were nonetheless deftly styled. Another complete restyle in 1965 brought flowing lines and a slight upward sweep to the rear quarter panels. This shape continued until 1969, when a replacement body introduced elliptical wheel openings, which were emphasized by subtle bulges. The prettiest big Chevrolet of the period might

1960 Chevrolet Impala Convertible

1962 Chevrolet Impala Sport Sedan

1961 Chevrolet Impala Two-Door Sedan

1963 Chevrolet Impala Convertible

1964 Chevrolet Impala Two-Door Hardtop

1967 Chevrolet Impala Sport Coupe

1965 Chevrolet Impala Two-Door Hardtop

1968 Chevrolet Impala Convertible

1965 Chevrolet Caprice Sport Sedan

1969 Chevrolet Impala Custom Coupe

be the 1962. It had straight, correct lines, and an interesting roofline with convertible-like "top bow" accents.

Among the big Chevrolets, Biscayne was the price leader. However, buyer interest in it fell during the decade. About 288,000 Biscaynes were built in 1960; only some 69,000 were produced in 1969. The Bel Air was the intermediate-priced large Chevrolet. Sales of this model also decreased: 382,000 were built in 1960; only 156,000 by 1969. The Impala, which had appeared as a "limited edition" car in 1958, had rapidly become the most popular model in the United States. It dominated sales of large Chevrolets. Its best year of the decade was 1964, when 889,600 units were built.

One Impala is worthy of particular attention—the performance-bred Super Sports model of 1965-67. Like the Corvair and Camaro, the Impala SS is already a Chevrolet collector's item.

The concept was simple: Take the big, 119-inch standard Chevrolet wheelbase, add a sporty body, and offer the car with options designed to enhance its performance and handling. The Impala SS was available only as a two-door hardtop and a convertible. A

six-cylinder engine was offered, but only 3,600 of the 243,100 cars built in 1965 were equipped with one. The standard specification called for the use of unique exterior badging and deleting the Impala's rocker panel brightwork. Vinyl bucket seats, a central console with gearshift lever, and options including a tachometer and sport steering wheel were added. Big Chevy V-8s were

1969 Chevrolet Kingswood Estate Wagon

Chevrolet

offered. (One of them displaced 409 cubic inches and developed 425 hp). And, equipped with an exciting list of handling options like stiffer springs and shocks, sintered metallic brake linings, four-speed gearbox, and ultra-quick power steering, an Impala SS became the highest-performance big Chevy in history. That's the way the car usually was outfitted.

But the Impala SS didn't last. Government regulations, a decline in demand for racing and race-bred automobiles, and the increased demand for smaller sporty cars all combined to do the Impala SS in after 1967. Production fell rapidly during the car's three model years. Meanwhile, Chevrolet had found a far more lucrative market by dolling up the Impala with the best grades of upholstery and trim, and calling the result "Caprice." This top-of-the-line Chevy arrived in 1966 and immediately captured 181,000 buyers.

Next in size in Chevrolet's model hierarchy of the

1964 Chevrolet Chevelle Malibu Four-Door Sedan

1962 Chevy II 300 Two-Door Sedan

1966 Chevrolet Chevelle SS Sport Coupe

1967 Chevy II Nova Super Sport Coupe

1967 Chevrolet Chevelle Sport Coupe

1968 Chevy II Nova Coupe

1969 Chevrolet Chevelle SS396 Sport Coupe

1969 Chevy Nova Coupe

'60s was the intermediate Chevelle, which was introduced in 1964 to compete against Ford's Fairlane. The Chevelle was conventional: front engine, rear-wheel drive, coil springs in front, leaf springs in the rear. It provided almost as much interior room as the Impala did, but had a more sensibly sized exterior. In effect it was a revival of the ideally proportioned, middle-wheelbase "classic" Chevrolets of 1955-57. Chevelle sales went nowhere but up, from 328,400 cars in its first year to nearly 440,000 by 1969. The addition of numerous performance options, and the Chevelle's own SS variations by 1965, enhanced the car's appeal.

Third in size among Chevrolets of the decade was the 110-inch-wheelbase Chevy II. It had been rushed into production for 1962 as a stopgap competitor to Ford's Falcon, which was handily trimming the Corvair in the compact car marketplace. The Corvair appealed to sporty-car fans, and the Falcon pleased the much broader field of compact buyers. Chevy IIs were available with a 153 cubic-inch four-cylinder engine of 90 hp, or a 194-cid 120-hp six. Falcons had only six-cylinder power plants.

Chevrolet hoped to outflank and outproduce Ford in this market segment. But through 1966, Chevy IIs outnumbered Falcons only once, in 1963. Between 1963 and 1964, sales of the Chevy II dropped nearly 50 percent, partly due to competition from the Chevelle. A series of Super Sport models didn't help. By the middle of the decade, it seemed that the Chevy II was destined for oblivion: production was only 106,500 units for 1967.

Then in 1968 the Chevy II received a new body, plus a 112-inch wheelbase for two-door models, and a 116 for four-doors. The new cars were known by the old top-line name of Nova. Backed by a strong ad campaign and competitive prices—one could be bought for about $2,300—the Chevy II Nova made a comeback. The division concentrated on only two body styles, a coupe and a four-door sedan, which sold as fast as they could be manufactured. By 1969 the Chevy II Nova was up to 270,000 units—its best year since 1963. As the Nova, it remained in production through 1979, when it was replaced by the front-wheel-drive Citation.

The Camaro is one of the more interesting and potentially the most collectible Chevrolet of the 1960s. Introduced in 1967, it was an immediate hit. Production topped 220,000 cars the first year, followed by 235,100 for 1968, and 243,100 for 1969.

The Camaro was born out of a need to replace the ailing Corvair. Despite the beautiful styling and impressive performance of the 1965 models, the Corvair had not threatened Ford's incredibly successful Mustang in the burgeoning market for "ponycars." Furthermore, the Corvair was expensive to build; it was entirely different in concept and technology from mainstream Chevrolet models. Six months after the 1965 Corvairs arrived, division managers decided to allow the rear-engine Chevy to fade out of production. To replace it, they planned a conventional front-engine sporty car—the ultimate solution to the Mustang.

The designing of the Camaro became the responsibility of William L. Mitchell, GM's vice-president of styling, and of the corporation's Styling Staff. There was no better team of designers in the industry than Mitchell's during this period. The look that resulted—a flat nose, a chiseled profile, a chopped-off deck, and a low roofline—was right. The Camaro appealed to those who wanted four-seaters with handling to match straight-line performance.

The Camaro was more than a new Chevrolet. It was a new concept. Ford's Mustang had pointed the way, and GM has never been reticent about borrowing good ideas. The Camaro offered 81 factory options and 41 dealer-installed accessories, allowing the buyer to tailor one to suit his taste and his budget. The car started with an f.o.b. price of $2,466 for the 140-hp six-cylinder coupe and $2,704 for the convertible. The 155-hp, 250 cubic-inch six cost $26 extra; the 210-hp 327 V-8 was an additional $106. Next on the list of available engines was a 350 cid V-8, which was an exclusive Camaro engine in 1967. Later it became the most popular Corvette power plant. This V-8 produced 295 hp. To get the engine, the buyer had to order the Super Sports package.

The SS option cost $211 and included a tight suspension (stiff springs and shocks), D70-14 Firestone Wide Oval tires, modified hood with insulation underneath, SS badging, and special hood striping. Early in the 1967 model year, the L-35 Chevrolet 396-cid V-8 (325 hp) and Turbo/Hydra-matic became available at a cost of nearly $400. Scores of other options tempted buyers: custom carpeting, bucket seats, fold-down back seat, a special interior group, floor-mounted shifters with console for the four-speed Turbo/Hydra-matic or heavy-duty three-speed, and full instrumentation. For $105, a Rally Sport package

1967 Chevrolet Camaro Sport Coupe

1968 Chevrolet Camaro Convertible

Chevrolet

added a hidden-headlight grille, special taillights and emblems, aluminum rocker moldings, black painted rocker bottoms, and miscellaneous trim. There were five different wheels and wheel covers, three types of steering wheels, headrests, shoulder belts, tinted glass, radios, heaters, air conditioning, clock, cruise control, and a vinyl-covered roof for hardtops. Mechanical options included sintered metallic brake linings, ventilated front disc brakes, vacuum brake booster, power steering, manual quick steering, stiff suspension, Positraction, and a dozen different axle ratios. Without too much trouble, the price for a Camaro could be boosted to $4,000 or even $5,000.

The Camaro wasn't significantly changed in 1968 or 1969, although interim face-lifts were proposed. The ultimate restyling was scheduled for 1970. The 1968 model received a new horizontal-texture grille, ventless side windows, and restyled taillights. The 1969 model had a slimmer body, lower front and rear wheel openings, a V-shaped grille, and new rear styling.

The big news in these years was the Z-28 Camaro, which won 18 of 25 Sports Car Club of America Trans-Am races and was Trans-Am sedan class champion in 1968 and 1969.

Vincent W. Piggins, veteran competition car engineer, had convinced Chevrolet management that a car should be built expressly for SCCA sedan racing. Piggins combined the 327 cubic-inch V-8 block with the 283 crankshaft to get a bore and stroke of 4x3 inches and a displacement of 302.4 cubic inches. Officially, this engine delivered 290 hp at 5800 rpm (actual bhp was more like 350), and 290 foot-pounds of torque at 4200 rpm. The 302 engine was coupled to a car having heavy-duty suspension, front disc brakes, metallic-lined rear drums, 11-inch clutch, close-ratio four-speed transmission with a 2.20:1 first gear, quick steering,

1969 Chevrolet Camaro Z-28

1969 Chevrolet Camaro Rally Sport Convertible

and wide Corvette wheels. It also had a restyled hood to increase carburetor air intake.

The Z-28 name came from the package's option number (not from Zora Arkus-Duntov, the famed Corvette engineer). In those days, you could buy a whale of an automobile for about $3,300. Few Z-28s were intended for the general public, of course; the object was to win the Trans-Am championship. But production quickly climbed, from 602 in 1967 to 7,199 in 1968 and 19,014 in 1969. The Z-28s are, of course, the ultimate performance Camaros. A decade or two from now, they should be one of the ultimate Chevrolet collector's items.

	1960	1961	1962	1963	1964	1965	1966	1967	1968	1969
CHEVROLET AT A GLANCE, 1960-1969										
Price Range, $	2175-2996	2175-3099	2003-3171	2003-3170	2011-3196	2011-3212	2090-3347	2090-3413	2222-3570	2237-3678
Weight Range, lbs.	3455-4000	3415-3930	2410-3925	2430-3870	2455-3895	2505-4005	2520-4020	2555-3990	2760-4005	2785-4300
Wheelbases, in.	119	119	110-119	110-119	110-119	110-119	110-119	108-119	108-119	108-119
4 Cyl. Engines, hp			90	90	90	90	90	90	90	90
6 Cyl. Engines, hp	135	135	120-135	120-140	120-140	120-140	120-155	120-155	140-155	140-155
8 Cyl. Engines, hp	170-315	170-315	170-409	195-425	195-425	195-425	195-425	195-385	200-425	200-425

Corvair
Chevrolet Division of General Motors Corp.
Detroit, Michigan

Chevrolet's Corvair project was full of ironies. The division had created an American Volkswagen with an air-cooled rear engine, efficient use of space, compact size, and excellent economy. Yet consumer advocates, who might have been expected to welcome such an automobile, disparaged it. This is not to say that Ralph Nader's book, *Unsafe at Any Speed,* singlehandedly killed the Corvair. Rather, the ax had actually fallen six months before Nader's book appeared. Bad press about the car's handling hurt. But economics played a part also. For General Motors, the Corvair never made it because it failed to compete well with Ford's Falcon as an economy car. (GM launched the Chevy II to fill the gap.) And, although Corvair started an automotive revolution with the sporty Monza, Ford's Mustang stole that market. Chevrolet was forced to react to, rather than to anticipate, Ford's actions.

Chevrolet's work on small rear-engine cars began after World War II, with a stillborn prototype called the Cadet. But postwar buyers were so hungry for cars, even warmed-over prewar models, that the division saw no need to build Cadets. By the late 1950s, however, the situation had changed radically. Imported cars, led by Volkswagen and Renault, were biting into the domestic market. The percentage of economy cars was becoming too large to ignore.

The first modern compact, Studebaker's 1959 Lark, was so successful that it temporarily halted Studebaker's slide into oblivion. The Lark soon had rivals. Ford laid plans for the Falcon, and Chrysler started work on the Valiant, both introduced as 1960 models. In 1958-59, General Motors had stemmed the tide with so-called "captive imports" like Vauxhall and Opel, but for 1960 GM pinned its hopes on the Corvair.

Largely the work of Edward N. Cole, longtime GM engineer (and future GM president), the Corvair was a technician's car, and by far the most radical of the three new compacts. Its power plant was a 140 cubic-inch flat six (bore and stroke 3.38 x 2.60 inches) that developed 80 to 95 horsepower. This engine was relatively complicated. It had two cylinder heads, six separate cylinder barrels, and a divided crankcase. Flat sixes were not common in automobiles; Corvair's power plant might have been inspired by Cole's interest in airplanes. Unfortunately, the production engine weighed 388 pounds, some 100 pounds more than the target weight. This miscalculation would have a negative effect on the car's handling.

The suspension of the 108-inch-wheelbase compact was basic—perhaps too basic. Up front were wishbones and coil springs; in the back were semi-trailing swing axles. There was no anti-sway bar, although GM had known this device to be one of several ways to achieve acceptable handling. Management's decision to reduce cost while maximizing ease of service and efficiency of assembly prevented the use of more sophisticated suspension components until 1962, when a regular production option including stiffer springs, shorter rear axle limit straps, and a front sway bar was made available. A major suspension improvement occurred in 1964, when a transverse compensating spring was adopted.

It should be pointed out, however, that the 1960-63 Corvair's rather basic four-wheel independent suspension did not create a "dangerous, ill-handling car," as lawsuits claimed. The car did oversteer, to be sure. But the oversteer was not excessive when tires were inflated to the proper pressures: 15 psi front, 26 psi rear. The point was argued for years, and was settled only by a congressional investigation, which found in the Corvair's favor. Drivers needed to pay strict attention to tire pressures. Some people did not do so.

The 10-year production run of the Chevrolet Corvair was divided into two segments: the first generation of 1960-64, and the second generation of 1965-69.

Corvairs were initially offered in three series. The 500 was the most basic package; the 700 was slightly

1961 Corvair Lakewood Station Wagon

1963 Corvair Monza Spyder Convertible

Corvair

better trimmed. Most interesting, though, was the 900—the Monza—with its deluxe interior and bucket seats. When Corvair offered an optional four-speed gearbox in 1961, Monza sales caught fire. A market that Chevrolet had not anticipated was revealed: a demand for sporty, fun-to-drive compact cars. This was fortunate, because the 500 and 700 series Corvairs were not competitive in price with the Falcon, and were being outsold by the Ford compact. By 1962 Monza sales were over 209,000, a figure that dominated Corvair production.

The most highly prized first-generation Corvair is the turbocharged Monza Spyder of 1962-64. Its 150-hp engine, multi-gauge instrument panel, host of handling and performance options, and coupe and convertible models made the Spyder a highly desirable automobile. Unfortunately, it wasn't cheap: the price was about $2,800 plus options. Production was limited to about 40,000 cars over three years.

For 1961, the flat six was bored out to 145 cubic inches, and optional horsepower went up to 102. In 1964, the engine was stroked for a displacement of 164 cubic inches (3.44 x 2.95 bore/stroke) and 95 to 110 hp in nonsupercharged form.

Another interesting first-generation Corvair was the Lakewood station wagon. The Lakewood appeared in 1961, and was a product of the years when economy was viewed as Corvair's greatest strength. It provided a surprising amount of cargo space—58 cubic feet behind the front seat, and 10 cubic feet under the hood. This was more than other compact wagons, and even more than some larger models. The wagon didn't sell well, however, and production barely topped 25,000 units in 1961. For 1962, the Lakewood name was dropped, and wagons were offered in both the 700 and Monza series. The Monza wagon was plush, equipped with bucket seats and deluxe trim. Only about 6,000 of the 1962 models were built before the wagon was dropped to make room on the assembly line for the hot Chevy II.

More popular than the wagon was the Corvair line of small trucks: the Greenbrier wagon, Rampside and Loadside pickups, and Corvan panel—all built on a 95-inch wheelbase. These vehicles, however, were not competitive with the rival Ford Econoline, and the last one was built in early 1965.

The sleek 1965 Corvairs were a design revolution. Good-looking, even from normally unflattering angles, they were a tribute to the fine edge honed on GM cars by styling chief William L. Mitchell and his designers. They looked almost like the work of an Italian coachbuilder. (In fact, Pininfarina built a 1964 Corvair with lines that were similar.) They were nicely shaped and not overdone, with just the right amount of trim.

Under the skin also, the 1965 Corvair was new. The turbocharged engine produced 180 hp at 4000 rpm,

1964 Corvair Monza Club Coupe

1966 Corvair Corsa Sport Coupe

1967 Corvair Monza Sport Sedan

1967 Corvair Monza Sport Sedan

making the turbo the most powerful stock Corvair power plant. But probably the best all-around Corvair engine was the new 140-hp version. New cylinder heads, redesigned manifolds, and four progressively linked carburetors gave it its extra power.

The 1960 Corvair had been the first mass-produced American car to offer swing-axle rear suspension. The 1965 Corvair was the first to offer fully independent suspension, discounting the Corvette. There was only one difference between the two: Corvette's rear suspension used a transverse leaf spring; Corvair's had a coil spring at each wheel. The rest of the system was the same: upper and lower control arms were used at each rear wheel. The uppers were actually the axle half-shafts; the lowers were unequal length, nonparallel bars. These four arms controlled all lateral wheel motion. Small rubber-mounted rods extended from each arm to the rear main cross-member to absorb shocks from movement at the trailing-arm pivot points.

No longer was there any question of tricky Corvair handling on hard corners. The camber of inside and outside wheels remained negative and produced maximum cornering force. The steering was nearly neutral, tending toward mild understeer at high speeds. The rear wheels, remaining at a constant angle with the ground, took most of the car's weight and enabled it to be pushed around corners at great speeds. Attention was also given to the front suspension, which was tuned to complement the rear suspension and to provide roll stiffness.

Of all second-generation cars, the 1965-66 Corsas were the most desirable. They came as sport coupes with a base price of $2,519 and convertibles at $2,665, complete with a full set of instruments, special exterior trim (including aluminum rear panel for instant identification), deluxe interior, and a 140-hp engine. The turbocharged six was a $158 option. With it, the Corsa was definitely in the high-performance category. A typical acceleration time was 0 to 60 mph in less than 11 seconds, and the car could do the standing-start quarter mile in 18 seconds at 80 mph. The Corsa could hit 115 mph when given enough straightaway. Yet it could deliver more than 20 miles per gallon at moderate highway speeds.

Unfortunately, the Corsa didn't sell particularly well against the Mustang, which could better the Chevy's performance. For the 1965 model year, Corsa production was 28,654 units; only 10,472 were produced for 1966, after which it was dropped. More critical was a decline in Monza sales. This most popular Corvair model rallied slightly in 1965, but the following year production plunged to about one-third the '65 level. By

1969 Corvair Monza Sport Coupe

that time, Nader's book was having an effect. But, according to Karl Ludvigsen in his history of Corvair, the car's fate already had been sealed by a GM directive in April, 1965: "No more development work," was the order," Do just enough to keep it up with the safety standards."

When Camaro was added to the sporty car lists for 1967, the Corvair line was trimmed to just two series: the 500 sedan and coupe; and the Monza sedan, coupe, and convertible. This was the last year for the Corvair hardtop sedans, which are collector's items today. Their production had reached 55,000 cars for 1965, but the total trailed off rapidly thereafter. The 1966 figure was 8,799 of the 500 model and 12,497 of the Monzas. For 1967, production reached only 2,959 of the 500 sedans and 3,157 Monzas.

The 1968-69 Corvairs were the rarest of the breed, available in just three body styles—500 hardtop, Monza coupe, and Monza convertible. These cars are readily identifiable by their front marker lights—clear lenses in 1968, amber ones in 1969. Monza convertibles were the scarcest models: production totaled 1,386 in 1968 and only 521 in 1969. They suffered from driveability problems, mainly due to an air pump that Chevrolet bolted on to keep them within emission limits.

It was obvious by 1968 that the Corvair was becoming an orphan. Some Chevrolet dealers wouldn't handle them, and others refused to service them. Cole's vision had faded, and Corvair died an undeserved death.

CORVAIR AT A GLANCE, 1960-1969										
	1960	1961	1962	1963	1964	1965	1966	1967	1968	1969
Price Range, $	1984-2238	1920-2331	1992-2846	1992-2798	2000-2811	2066-2665	2083-2662	2128-2540	2243-2626	2258-2641
Weight Range, lbs.	2270-2315	2320-2555	2350-2625	2330-2525	2365-2580	2385-2710	2400-2720	2435-2695	2470-2725	2515-2770
Wheelbases, in.	108	108	108	108	108	108	108	108	108	108
6 Cyl. Engines, hp	80-95	80-102	80-150	80-150	95-150	95-180	95-180	95-140	95-140	95-140

Corvette

**Chevrolet Division of General Motors Corp.
Detroit, Michigan**

For 1960, the Corvette, Chevrolet's sports car, was substantially the same as it had been in 1958-59—flashy and fast. But there was an increase in the use of aluminum: in the clutch housing, the radiator, and the cylinder heads of fuel-injected engines. (The aluminum heads performed poorly in the field, and were soon discontinued.) The 1960 Corvette also featured anti-sway bars front and rear, which greatly improved ride and handling. It was the first use of a rear sway bar on an American car.

In that year, Corvette achieved international recognition in the 24-hour race at Le Mans in France. Three cars were entered by Briggs Cunningham in the GT class. They all performed exceptionally well, and one hit 151 miles an hour on the Mulsanne Straight. A Corvette finished eighth overall in this race, the toughest of all international endurance contests.

The 1960-61 period was the last in which Corvette's 283 cubic-inch V-8 was used. During those two years, six variations of the 283 engine were offered. They ranged from a single four-barrel-carburetor engine with 230 horsepower to a fuel-injected version with 315 hp. A wide assortment of rear axle ratios and three transmission choices (three-speed, four-speed, and automatic) were available. As in the past, it was possible to tailor a Corvette to very specific requirements, from boulevard touring to all-out competition.

Styling for 1961-62 was a mild face-lift of the 1960 model, but a highly effective one. The cars retained the basic 1958-60 front end and midsection, but were completely restyled at the rear. By that time, William L. Mitchell had relieved Harley Earl as chief of design at General Motors, and the new rear end treatment was Mitchell's idea. It was a ducktail shape derived from the

racing Stingray and the experimental XP-700.

Corvette prices climbed in the early 1960s. The list price went from $3,875 to $4,038 between 1960 and 1962. Fuel-injected, fully equipped cars could cost more than $5,000.

Engine and gearbox options for 1961 were unchanged from 1960. More than 85 percent of Corvette buyers ordered manual transmission, and more than half of them requested the four-speed. The 315-hp engine was most impressive when coupled to stump-pulling rear axle ratios. With the 4.11:1 ratio, for example, the 315 could accelerate from 0 to 60 in 5.5 seconds and cover the standing quarter mile in 14.2 seconds at 99 mph. Despite this tall numerical ratio, the car could approach a top speed of 130 mph.

For 1962, Mitchell further refined Corvette styling. De-emphasizing the concave side molding, he eliminated its chrome outline. He also replaced the "teeth" inside the reverse scoop with a grid. The grille was blacked out, and a decorative strip of anodized aluminum was added to the rocker panels. Also in '62, stiff springs were brought back as an option. Dr. Richard Thompson won the Sports Car Club of America A-production championship that year in a Corvette so equipped.

After Semon E. "Bunkie" Knudsen became Chevrolet's general manager in 1962, the Corvette was slated for increased production. Chevrolet built 14,531 Corvettes that year, up from 10,939 units in 1961. Corvette had turned the profit corner in 1958 and was seeing an adequate return on investment. Production continued to increase in the years that followed.

In 1962, a new 327 cubic-inch V-8, created by enlarging the 283 to a 4.00 x 3.25-inch bore and stroke,

1961 Corvette Convertible

was introduced. The fuel-injection system was also modified. A 3.08:1 rear axle ratio was used for quieter cruising with the two lowest-horsepower engines.

The 327 V-8 was the basic Corvette power plant through 1965. In 1962-63, it was available in four versions: 250-340 hp with carburetion, and 360-395 hp with fuel injection. Improved torque gave the 327 with the 3.70:1 rear axle ratio the capability to run the quarter mile in 15 seconds at more than 100 mph. And, with its new optional sintered metallic brake linings, the Corvette could stop as well as it could go. In SCCA racing, it was undisputed champion in both A-production and B-production classes, and it competed in good form at Sebring.

The 1963 Sting Ray was revolutionary. It was a complete revision—the first complete remake—of Chevrolet's sports car, which had remained mostly unchanged between 1953 and 1962. The only items carried over from 1962 were the engines. In addition to the Sting Ray roadster, there was a beautiful grand touring coupe, and more than 10,500 copies of each body style were sold. Both new models were unquestionably landmark designs.

Prototypes for what became the 1963 Corvette began appearing in late 1959. The first of these cars was the experimental XP-720. Based on the Stingray racer, this coupe featured a smooth fastback fuselage that was set off by a distinctive split rear window. The divided rear window was Mitchell's idea, but it appeared only for 1963. He was disappointed when it was replaced for 1964 by a single piece of glass.

The XP-720 package was practical as well as attractive. Early alterations from the Stingray racer included hidden headlights, achieved through the use of pivoting sections that were flush with the creased front end. The styling included an attractive dip in the beltline at the upper trailing edge of the doors. The doors of the coupe were cut into the roof. The Corvette's new "dual cockpit" dashboard was a fresh approach that worked remarkably well.

After the XP-720 was firmed up, a roadster version was developed. A four-passenger Corvette was considered too, but the idea was dropped because it seemed out of character. Final prototypes were intensively evaluated. Wind tunnel tests were made to determine aerodynamics. Body engineers added as well as subtracted weight. As a result, the 1963 model had almost twice as much steel support as the 1962 Corvette in its central body structure, but less fiberglass in its body.

The 1963 Corvette Sting Ray had a shorter wheelbase than the 1962 model—only 98 inches. Its rear track was two inches narrower. The frontal area was reduced by one square foot. Interior space, however, was at least as good in every direction. And, thanks to the added steel reinforcement, the cockpit was made stronger and safer than before.

Compared to the '62 model, the '63 was a superior car. There was no change in engines from the previous year, but the chassis was reworked, primarily at the rear. The fully independent rear suspension was a

Corvette Stingray Racing Prototype

1963 Corvette Sting Ray Sport Coupe

1963 Corvette Sting Ray Convertible

1964 Corvette Sting Ray Sport Coupe

1964 Corvette Sting Ray Sport Coupe

Corvette

three-link type with double-jointed open drive shafts at either side, control arms, and trailing radius rods. A single transverse leaf spring was mounted to the frame with rubber-cushioned struts. In accord with the wishes of leading Corvette engineer Zora Arkus-Duntov, the differential was bolted to the rear cross-member. The frame itself was a well-reinforced box. Weight distribution was 48/52, compared to the previous 53/47. The '63's ride and handling were significantly better than that of the '62. A new recirculating-ball steering gear, combined with a dual-arm, three-link ball-joint front suspension made the steering quicker. The front brake drums were wider, and all brakes were self-adjusting. The car had an alternator instead of a generator, positive crankcase ventilation, a smaller flywheel, and a new aluminum clutch housing. Competition options included stiff suspension, metallic brake linings, cast aluminum knock-off wheels, and a 36.5-gallon long-distance fuel tank.

Corvette styling became cleaner through the five years of the Sting Ray generation. In 1964 its fake hood louvers were dropped, and the coupe's rear quarter vents were made functional. In 1965, the hood panel was smoothed and the front fender slots were opened. By 1967, the cars had reached a peak in styling, and the only changes were an oblong back-up light, bolt-on instead of knock-off aluminum wheels, revised front fender louvers, and optional vinyl covering for the roadster's removable hardtop roof.

Mechanically, important advancements were made through the mid-1960s. The new fuel-injected, 375-hp small-block engine of 1963 developed 1.15 hp per cubic inch. For 1965, Corvettes were equipped with disc brakes on all four wheels, and the new Mark IV engine which developed 425 hp.

The first Mark IV displaced 396 cubic inches, but it was increased to 427 in 1967. To handle its brute force, Chevrolet used a stiff suspension, a heavy clutch, and a large radiator and fan. With the 4.11:1 rear axle ratio, a 1966 Mark IV could go from 0 to 60 in less than five seconds and attain more than 140 mph. Fuel injection was dropped after 1965 for the smaller engines. This was mainly due to high cost and low sales. Carbureted 327 V-8s during this period ranged from 250 to 350 hp; injection engines offered 360 to 395 hp.

Chevrolet had considered building a mid-engine Corvette for 1968, but the high cost of the transaxle prohibited the car's production. Instead, there was a complete restyling, chiefly the work of the division's design studio under David Holls. The 1968 model was an aggressive, swoopy-looking car with an air dam at the front and a spoiler at the rear. Its aerodynamic properties, however, were not especially good. A roadster and a notchback hardtop were offered. Pop-up hidden headlights and concealed windshield

1966 Corvette Sting Ray Sport Coupe

1967 Corvette Sting Ray Sport Coupe

1968 Corvette Sport Coupe

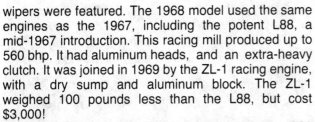

1968 Corvette Convertible

1969 Corvette Stingray Sport Coupe

wipers were featured. The 1968 model used the same engines as the 1967, including the potent L88, a mid-1967 introduction. This racing mill produced up to 560 bhp. It had aluminum heads, and an extra-heavy clutch. It was joined in 1969 by the ZL-1 racing engine, with a dry sump and aluminum block. The ZL-1 weighed 100 pounds less than the L88, but cost $3,000!

The Sting Ray name had disappeared on 1968 models, but it was back— as one word—on the 1969s. These cars were improved in detail. The exterior door handles were cleaner than those of the 1968s, black-painted grille bars replaced the chrome, and the back-up lights were integrated with inner taillights. Handling was improved by wide rim wheels, and the frame was stiffened. The interior was revised to create more room for passengers and their equipment. The 327 engine was stroked to 350 cubic inches (bore and stroke 4.00 x 3.48 inches), and was offered with either 300 or 350 hp. Four 427 engines were also available, with an array of axle ratios from 4.56:1 to 2.75:1.

The 1968 package, however, was not received with unanimous praise, and debate surrounds it to the present day. *Road & Track* magazine summed up the case for the opposition, saying that the car was "highly reminiscent of certain older Ferraris, laid around a chassis that seemed fairly modern in 1962 but is now quite dated by the march of progress . . . we feel that the general direction of the change is away from Sports Car and toward image and gadget car."

The new Corvette body was seven inches longer than that of its predecessor, mostly in front overhang. Its wheelbase was unchanged at 98 inches, but the interior was more cramped, and there was less luggage space. About 150 pounds had been added to what *Road & Track* called the "already gross avoirdupois." It was a great machine, the magazine said, "for those who like their cars big, flashy and full of blinking lights and trap doors. . . . The connoisseur who values finesse, efficiency and the latest chassis design will have to look, unfortunately, to Europe."

Although the 1963-67 Sting Ray is considered the classic Corvette of the '60s, the 1968-69 models were more successful with the public. The production peak was set in 1969, with 38,762 units—a record that would stand until 1976. The 1968-69 models were longer, heavier, and clumsier than their predecessors, but they were still very fast and appealing. They remained America's only true sports cars. "Corvettes are for driving, by drivers," *Car Life* magazine said. "The Corvette driver will be tired of smiling long before he's tired of the car."

CORVETTE AT A GLANCE, 1960-1969										
	1960	1961	1962	1963	1964	1965	1966	1967	1968	1969
Price Range, $	3875	3934	4038	4037-4252	4037-4252	4106-4321	4084-4295	4141-4353	4320-4663	4438-4781
Weight Range, lbs.	2840	2905	2925	2859-2881	2945-2960	2975-2985	2985-3005	3000-3020	3055-3065	3140-3145
Wheelbases, in.	102	102	102	98	98	98	98	98	98	98
8 Cyl. Engines, hp	230-315	230-315	250-395	250-395	250-395	250-425	300-425	300-435	300-435	300-435

Chrysler

Chrysler Division of Chrysler Corp.
Highland Park, Michigan

Chrysler advertising during the 1960s had a strident, almost belligerent tone. The company repeatedly declared that there would never be a small Chrysler. (Of course there would be, when the time was right and the government would allow little else.) In the early '60s, as rival manufacturers were rushing compact models into production, Chrysler capitalized on the fact that it was doing no such thing. Dodge and Plymouth divisions could handle compacts; but Chryslers would always be the large, brawny, luxurious cars they'd traditionally been. So it remained through the end of the decade.

The 1960-61 Chryslers were the last outlandishly plumed creations of Virgil Exner, father of the tail fin. In the vernacular of the time, they were clean designs—uncluttered with excess chrome, and fitted with lots of glass and an aggressive, inverted trapezoid grille. Detail improvements for 1960 included four-way hazard flashers and optional swivel seats that pivoted outward through an automatic latch release when a door was opened.

The engines used were two big, wedge-head V-8s. Windsors and Saratogas used a 383 cubic-inch version (bore and stroke 4.03 x 3.75 inches) that produced 305 horsepower in the Windsor and 325 hp in the Saratoga. New Yorkers and the limited-edition 300F used a 413-cid engine (4.18 x 3.75), which developed 350 hp in the New Yorker and 380 hp in the 300F. The last year for the Chrysler Saratoga was 1960, when only 15,525 were built. The Windsor lasted only through 1961. Then came the attractive Newport, which was Chrysler's volume car from 1961 into the '70s. Newports were competitively priced at just under $3,000 through 1964, and Chrysler's advertising emphasized this point. A Chrysler priced at less than $3,000 was exciting to many people. Newport sales soared; they exceeded 125,000 units by 1965.

The larger-engine Chryslers included six varieties of New Yorker: sedans, hardtops, convertibles, and wagons, priced from $4,409 to $5,022. Chrysler's luxury series, the New Yorker, sold at a rate of about 20,000 units a year in those days. It was priced just under the Imperial, competitively with the larger Buicks.

The most exciting of all Chryslers in 1960 was the sixth edition of the "letter series" 300, the 300F. It combined racy styling with a road-hugging suspension and an optional Pont-a-Mousson four-speed gearbox. A set of ram-induction manifolds boosted the output of its 413-cid V-8 to 375 hp. The 300F would do the standing quarter mile in 16 seconds at 85 mph. It rode hard, but cornered better than any other car of its size. A half dozen different axle ratios could be ordered. (Using the 3.03 ratio, special tuning and some stream-lining, Andy Granatelli came close to 190 mph for the

flying mile.) The 300F came as a hardtop priced at $5,411, and a convertible priced at $5,841. They weren't cheap, but they offered a lot of performance for the money.

The 1960 models were significant in that they were the first unit-body Chryslers. This configuration replaced the traditional type, built by attaching a body to a frame with flexible mountings. Since unit bodies were held together more by welds than by nuts and bolts,

1960 Chrysler New Yorker Convertible

1961 Chrysler 300G Two-Door Hardtop

1961 Chrysler New Yorker Town and Country Wagon

they were not prone to looseness or rattles, but they were susceptible to rust.

The 1961 line was mostly a repeat of the 1960, except for the advent of the Newport and the discontinuation of the Saratoga. The Newport was equipped with a smaller engine, the 361 cubic-inch V-8 (4.12 x 3.38), which developed 265 hp. The 300G did not use the 300F's optional four-speed French gearbox, but a floor-mounted three-speed. The letter series also returned to 15-inch wheels, for the first time since 1956. Two engines were offered for this series. They produced 375 and 400 hp. Both power plants had ram-induction.

Management changes during 1961 had an immediate effect on Chrysler products. At the end of July, corporate president Lester Lum "Tex" Colbert retired under fire. Colbert had turned the presidency over to his chosen successor, William Newberg. But Newberg quit after two months, when he was found to have financial interests in several of Chrysler's suppliers. Lynn A. Townsend, former administrative vice-president, utlimately replaced Colbert. In 1967, Townsend became board chairman. Chrysler's president from January 1967 to January 1970 was Virgil Boyd.

This shakeup brought with it a new styling head. Exner had departed in 1961, though he had already shaped the 1962-64 models. His replacement was Elwood Engle, former Ford designer and creator of the elegant 1961 Lincoln Continental. Engle was responsible for the Chryslers of 1965 on. So the mid-1960s were years of change for Chrysler styling. For 1962, the division fielded what Exner called the "plucked chicken": a conservative model much like the 1961, but without the tail fins. The 1963-64 cars had what Chrysler called "the crisp, clean custom look." They were chiseled, chunky cars that had been designed just before Exner departed. Then in 1965, Engle unveiled his smooth, concave-sided models. (Their fenders were edged with bright metal, which, used in this way, was an Engle trademark.) This shape governed Chrysler's appearance into 1969, when Engle redesigned the cars and came up with a more rounded, less bulky shape.

For 1962 the Windsor was dropped, but Chrysler maintained its three-model lineup with the "non-letter" 300s. These were sporty-looking cars having fashionable features such as a center console and bucket seats. They were offered as hardtops or convertibles. The 300s were popular. About 25,000 units were sold each year through 1965.

The New Yorker rode a 126-inch wheelbase; all other Chryslers in 1962 had a wheelbase of 122 inches. In 1963-64, however, all Chryslers adopted the 122-inch wheelbase, which made the New Yorker the same general size as less expensive models. This did not hamper New Yorker sales, which were strong in both years. Two special models in this period were the 300 Pace Setter, two-door hardtops and convertibles; and New Yorker Salon, a four-door hardtop sedan. The Pace Setter commemorated the pacing of the 1963 Indianapolis 500 by a Chrysler. It was identified by

crossed, checkered flags and special trim. Its price was $3,769 to $4,129. The New Yorker Salon sold for $5,860. It came with such standard luxury accessories as air conditioning; AM/FM radio; auto-pilot; power brakes, steering, seats, and windows; TorqueFlite automatic transmission; color-keyed wheel covers; and vinyl-covered roof. The same basic lineup of Chryslers continued for 1964.

The 1963-64 300J and 300K (they skipped the letter "I" to avoid confusion with the number "1") were big, hefty cars in the tradition of the letter series. They came only as hardtops. Only 400 of the 300Js were built in '63 (an all-time low), but production of 300Ks increased to 3,647 for 1964. The 1965 version, the 300L, was the last of the letter series, though the range

1962 Chrysler 300 Two-Door Hardtop

1963 Chrysler 300J Two-Door Hardtop

1964 Chrysler New Yorker Salon Four-Door Hardtop

Chrysler

expanded again to a hardtop coupe and convertible. Production of 300Ls totaled 440 convertibles and 2,405 coupes. The 1963-65 letter-series cars weren't quite the potent machines their predecessors had been, but they did have tight suspensions and were the most roadable Chryslers in the lineup. Engine options included power plants of up to 390 horsepower in 1963-64. The most power available in 1965 was 360 hp. The letter series was discontinued after 1965 because of low volume. Chrysler successfully attracted a clientele of sporty-car fans with its "non-letter" 300. The 1965 Newport graduated to the 383 V-8.

All Chrysler models did well in 1965 and 1966. The division built 125,795 Newports, 27,678 300s, and 49,871 New Yorkers in '65. In '66, sales were even better. Production of the 300s nearly doubled, and Newport production rose by 42,000 units.

The Engle Chryslers of 1965-69 were shorter than their predecessors, but just as big inside. The wheelbase of all models except wagons was 124 inches, up two inches from 1964. The wagons rode a 121-inch

1964 Chrysler 300 Two-Door Hardtop

1965 Chrysler Newport Four-Door Sedan

1966 Chrysler New Yorker Four-Door Hardtop

wheelbase in 1965-66, and a 122-inch thereafter.

During the late 1960s, the Chrysler range grew. The Newport was joined in '67 by a Newport Custom, which was priced about $200 higher than the regular Newport. Promoted as "a giant step in luxury, a tiny step in price," the Custom series comprised a two-door and a four-door hardtop, and a four-door sedan. The cars' deluxe interiors included jacquard upholstery, textured vinyl, and pull-down center armrests. The instrumentation of a fully equipped Newport Custom included eight toggle switches, three thumb wheels, 16 push buttons, three sliding levers and 12 other controls that, as Chrysler brochures proclaimed, "put you in charge of almost every option in the book." It was the ultimate in gadgetry. Vinyl-covered lift handles were used on the trunk. And there were "over 1,000 chrome accents along the sides, plus 15 gold crown medallions," according to the brochure.

Chrysler wagons went through many changes during the late '60s. The luxurious New Yorker Town & Country was dropped after 1965 (only 3,000 units had been sold that year). During 1966-68, all the wagons carried the Newport name. All-vinyl upholstery was used in the wagons instead of the cloth and vinyl of the Newport sedans. Standard features of the wagons included power steering, power brakes, and automatic transmission. Town & Countrys could accommodate up to nine passengers. The wagon's unique three-in-one front seat looked like a conventional bench, but each half could be adjusted to the front and rear individually, and the seat back on the passenger's side could be lowered. For 1969, the Town & Country became a separate series in its own right, and nearly 25,000 units were sold that model year.

Midyear specials were the focus of the spring 1968 selling season. A flashy Newport was offered with Sportsgrain simulated wood paneling like that of the wagons. (Sportsgrain was a $126 option for hardtops and convertibles.) Newport Special two-door and four-door hardtops were available with turquoise color schemes. These colors were later extended to the 300 series.

A record for calendar year production had been set in 1968, as more than 263,000 units were built. But the fuselage-styled 1969s didn't do as well: Calendar year production was only 226,590 units. This caused Chrysler to drop from 10th to 11th place in calendar year production. Yet the '69s were handsome. They sported a combination bumper and grille, clean lines, and no sign of tail fins. If not the most beautiful Chryslers of the decade, they were close rivals to the good-looking '62s and '65s.

Chrysler de-emphasized high performance in the last years of the 1960s. The 383 cubic-inch V-8 offered on Newports and Town & Countrys had only one state of tune: 290 hp. The 413-cid power plant for the New Yorker and 300 was replaced in 1969 by a 440-cid engine of 350 hp, with a 375-hp option.

Chrysler's wheelbase remained at 124 inches in 1969, but the cars kept growing, to almost 225 inches long and nearly 80 inches wide—about as big as the

1967 Chrysler New Yorker Four-Door Hardtop

1968 Chrysler Newport Custom Two-Door Hardtop

1968 Chrysler 300 Two-Door Hardtop

1969 Chrysler Newport Custom Four-Door Hardtop

1968 Chrysler Newport Two-Door Hardtop

1969 Chrysler Town and Country Wagon

American passenger car would get.

Vast changes were also evident in the company's administration by 1969. Quality control had become an end in itself for the first time in Chrysler history, as engineers struggled to improve the cars' reputation for poor body durability. The number of company-owned dealerships was increasing. The old centralized corporate structure had been decentralized under Colbert, but Townsend recentralized it. Townsend did retain division identity between the Chrysler-Plymouth and Dodge marques. Chrysler as a marque would face tough sledding in the early 1970s, as the division's decision not to sell a small car would begin to cause problems.

CHRYSLER AT A GLANCE, 1960-1969										
	1960	1961	1962	1963	1964	1965	1966	1967	1968	1969
Price Range, $	3194-5841	2964-5843	2964-5461	2964-5860	2901-5860	3009-4827	3052-4233	3159-4339	3306-4500	3414-4615
Weight Range, lbs.	3815-4535	3690-4455	3690-4445	3760-4370	3760-4395	4000-4745	3875-4550	3920-4550	3850-4410	3891-4485
Wheelbases, in.	122-126	122-126	122-126	122	122	121-124	121-124	122-124	122-124	122-124
8 Cyl. Engines, hp	305-380	265-400	265-380	265-390	265-390	270-360	270-350	270-350	290-350	290-375

Continental

Lincoln-Mercury Division of Ford Motor Co.
Dearborn, Michigan

There's been plenty of confusion over when Continental was a make and when it was merely a model of Lincoln. The Continental made during the 1940-48 period, belatedly named "Mark I," was a Lincoln model. There were no Continentals in 1949-55. The 1956-57 Continental Mark II, however, was a make: Ford formed a separate division to produce the car. The Mark III, IV, and V cars of 1958-60 were also Continentals. Then came a hiatus in the Mark series. Beginning in 1961, the division produced a series of Lincoln Continentals. In 1968, however, Ford introduced another Mark III. So the Mark III, IV, and V cars of the late 1960s and 1970s are technically Continentals, not Lincolns.

The 1960 Continental Mark V represented the last vestige of Ford's super-car program, which had begun in 1956 with the Continental Mark II. The Mark II never sold well at its $10,000 price, so in 1958 it was replaced by the Mark III series of lower-priced sedans, hardtops, and convertibles. The Mark IV, which consisted of six models including a limousine and a formal sedan, appeared in 1959. This lineup was repeated in 1960 as the Continental Mark V.

The 1960 Mark V shared its long 131-inch wheelbase with the 1960 Lincoln and Lincoln Premiere but was priced about $900 higher than the Premiere, model for model. For $6,845, a Mark V buyer had the option of a pillarless or pillar-type four-door sedan; a hardtop coupe cost $6,598. The Mark V convertible was priced at $7,058, the formal sedan sold for $9,208, and the limousine cost $10,230. The 1958-60 Continentals sold much better than had the Mark II, though annual volume never exceeded 13,000 units. They cost considerably more than long-wheelbase Cadillac 60 Specials, but less than Eldorados. In a sense, these Continentals had their own special market, and for Lincoln, a 13,000-unit sale was not to be ignored.

Production during 1960 heavily favored the Mark V four-door hardtop. Just 6,604 units were made. Also produced were 2,044 convertibles, 1,461 hardtop coupes, 807 four-door sedans, 136 formal sedans, and 34 limousines. The engine used was the 430 cubic-inch Lincoln V-8 (bore and stroke of 4.30 x 3.70 inches), which developed 315 hp. The cars were fast both off the line and at top speed, but because they weighed more than two and a half tons, handling was clumsy; they were designed strictly for cruising. Attempts had been made to maintain the aura of Mark II quality: Leather upholstery and a long list of power equipment contributed to the Mark V's air of exclusivity. But in style it was not of the same league as the Mark II, and the company realized this. So a new Lincoln Continental sedan and convertible was introduced in 1961.

The Lincoln Continentals of 1961-67 were successful. Production reached 25,000 units in 1961, and had more than doubled by 1966. Sales were higher than Lincoln had achieved in the 1950s, and enabled the company to reconsider the original Continental theme.

Classic automobiles, it seems, are never quite forgotten. During the early '60s, Ford executives, engineers, stylists, and dealers longed for another Continental in the tradition of the original car and the Mark II. The answer was the 1968 Continental Mark III.

The new Continental, according to Ford Motor Company, was the car most closely linked to Henry Ford II. Just as his brother William Clay had influenced the early Mark II and as his father Edsel had sponsored the Mark I, Henry Ford II insured that the 1968 Continental Mark III was a reflection of his personal taste in automobiles. Why was the Mark III name used again, instead of the more logical Mark VI? The reason is that Henry Ford II viewed the heavyweight 1958-60 cars as unworthy of the Continental marque. As a result, company promotion ballyhooed the 1968 Continental as a direct descendant of the Mark I and II.

1960 Continental Mark V Four-Door Hardtop

1968 Continental Mark III

The 1968 Mark III entered the product-planning stage in late 1965. From the beginning the goal was clear. It was to be a personal luxury car that had a long hood and short deck, in the traditional Continental image. Styling was supervised by chief designer Eugene Bordinat. Hermann Brunn (namesake of the great coachbuilder) was a member of Bordinat's staff, and was largely responsible for the car's interior. The junior Brunn designed large, comfortable bucket seats and a wood-grained dashboard with easy-to-reach controls. Henry Ford II selected the car's final shape from a number of designs submitted by Ford stylists in early 1966.

The Mark III was finally ready by April 1968. Because of its late introduction, only 7,770 units were built that year. But there was no question about the car's rightness for the market. In 1969, more than 23,000 Mark IIIs were sold.

The Mark III was set on a 117.2-inch wheelbase, which was nine inches shorter than that of the Continental Mark II of 1956-57. The $6,585 Mark III, however, was the same length as the Cadillac Eldorado, which sold for $6,608. Although the front-wheel-drive Eldroado was technologically more advanced, the Continental seemed to have more magic to its name. In sales it virtually matched the Eldorado during its four-year lifespan, and never trailed by more than 2,000 units a year. This was a significant achievement, because the entire range of Lincoln cars had never come close to matching Cadillac production.

The Mark III was powered by a 460 cubic-inch (4.36 x 3.85) V-8 with 10.5:1 compression and 365 brake horsepower at 4600 rpm, one of the industry's largest engines. It was a good-looking car, with the longest hood—more than six feet—of any American automobile. It also had clean lines, and a buyer had a wide choice of luxury interiors and special exteriors. Customers could choose from 26 exterior colors, including four special "Moondust" metallic paints. The price of the 1969 Mark III increased to $6,758, but there were no other changes in the car. Standard features on all Mark IIIs included Select-Shift Turbo Drive automatic transmission, power brakes (disc brakes in front, drum brakes in the rear), concealed headlights, ventless side windows, power seats, power windows, flow-through ventilation, and 150 pounds of sound-deadening insulation.

1968 Continental Mark III

1969 Continental Mark III

1969 Continental Mark III

CONTINENTAL AT A GLANCE, 1960-1969										
	1960	1961	1962	1963	1964	1965	1966	1967	1968	1969
Price Range, $	6,598-10,230								6585	6758
Weight Range, lbs.	4967-5500								4739	4762
Wheelbases, in.	131								117.2	117.2
8 Cyl. Engines, hp	315								365	365

DeSoto

Plymouth-DeSoto-Valiant Division of Chrysler Corp.
Detroit, Michigan

The DeSoto was discontinued in 1961 after 33 years of production. Originally, the car was intended to fit into a price niche between Dodge and Chrysler, but by the early 1960s Dodge and Chrysler models were competing in DeSoto's market.

DeSoto's demise was hastened by an adjustment in Chrysler's marketing approach. In the past there had been three types of dealers: Chrysler-Plymouth, De-Soto-Plymouth, and Dodge-Plymouth. The advent of Imperial in 1955 prompted Chrysler Division to concentrate on the lower end of its market, while larger and more luxurious Dodge models increased Dodge Division's spread upward. Both Chrysler and Dodge ate into DeSoto's territory. Then, in 1958, a recession crippled car sales, particularly in DeSoto's price range. Rumors of DeSoto's imminent demise were heard as early as 1959, and they naturally affected sales.

The statistics were ominous. Although calendar year production had increased slightly in 1959 over 1958, the volume for both years was less than half that of 1957, when DeSoto had built nearly 120,000 cars. DeSoto, of course, was in the same kind of trouble as many other middle-priced cars, including Oldsmobile, Buick, and Mercury. But those makes had higher volume and could stand to lose more money. Fur-

thermore, all of them had compact models ready for introduction in 1961. Although DeSoto's plans for 1962 included downsized standard models, there was no program for a compact.

Initially, rumors of a discontinuation of the DeSoto marque were strongly denied. In 1959, a celebration was held to mark the division's two-millionth car. Press releases noted that there were almost one million DeSotos still registered. And the division announced that $25 million would be invested in the engineering and styling of future cars, $7 million of which would be earmarked for the 1960 models. DeSoto officials said that commitments had been made for 1961, and work on 1962-63 models was in the development stage. It was also pointed out that Chrysler had regularly made a profit on DeSoto cars.

In 1960, however, Chrysler merged DeSoto and Plymouth into one division, and added Valiant, which was ostensibly a separate make. Valiant did very well and Plymouth did fairly well, but DeSoto fared poorly. During the first two months of 1960, DeSoto sales totaled 4,746, or 0.51 percent of the industry's new-car total. This was much less than the sales in the first two months of 1959, when the figures were 6,134 units and 0.72 percent. By the end of 1960, plans for the restyled

1960 DeSoto Adventurer Four-Door Hardtop

1960 DeSoto Adventurer Four-Door Sedan

1961 DeSoto Two-Door Hardtop

1962 DeSoto models had been shelved, and the 1961 models, announced in October 1960, were taken off the market. DeSoto-Plymouth dealers became Chrysler-Plymouth agencies, to the chagrin of existing Chrysler-Plymouth dealers in their areas.

DeSoto's range of models was reduced appreciably in 1960. During 1957-59, there had been four separate series, ranging from the low-priced Firesweep to the limited-production Adventurer. After 1957, all suffered from declining sales. For 1960, the range was reduced to two series, each with three models: sedan, hardtop sedan, and hardtop coupe. The Adventurer took the place of the DeSoto Fireflite, though its price was a few hundred dollars less than the 1959 Fireflite. The Fireflite was moved down into the $3,000 range that had been occupied by the Firesweep. Both the Firesweep and the mid-priced Firedome were eliminated. Station wagons and convertibles were dropped. The most popular DeSoto was the Fireflite sedan, production of which reached 9,032 units; and the Adventurer sedan, of which 5,746 were built. The rarest were four-door hardtops: 2,759 Adventurers and 1,958 Fireflites. As for two-door hardtops, there were 3,494 Fireflites and 3,092 Adventurers.

The 1960 DeSoto rode a 122-inch wheelbase, which it shared with Chrysler. And like the Chrysler's, its body and frame were built in one welded unit. Adventurers used the Chrysler 383 cubic-inch V-8 (bore and stroke 4.25 x 3.38 inches), with the same compression but 305 bhp at 4600 rpm. Automatic transmission, either Powerflite or Torqueflite, was optional on Fireflite models. The car had a blunt, trapezoidal grille composed of small horizontal bars, which was carried over a huge, curved bumper and protected by rubber-capped bumper guards. Tail fins were as high as they'd ever been on a Chrysler product, and the glass area was huge. The 1960 DeSotos were mediocre in performance. The Adventurer's specification duplicated the Chrysler Windsor's: the Fireflite's V-8 was borrowed from Dodge. In a drag race, the Adventurer could stay with a Windsor, but would lose to Saratoga or a 383 cubic-inch V-8 Dodge Phoenix, which was lighter than the DeSoto.

The brief appearance of the 1961 DeSoto resulted in low production figures: 2,123 hardtop sedans; 911 hardtop coupes. No series names were used; the cars were simply DeSotos. The four-door pillared sedan was eliminated from the lineup. Publicity concentrated on the individuality of the cars. The 1961 models were considered ugly, having a double grille and diagonally stacked headlights. A lattice-like lower grille was surmounted by a large, blunt oval bearing the nameplate against a smaller mesh. DeSoto production tapered off by Christmas 1960, and existing orders were filled mostly with Chrysler Windsors.

The 1961 DeSotos were a sad finale for a marque that had brought Chrysler considerable prestige and profits for more than three decades.

DESOTO AT A GLANCE, 1960-1969										
	1960	1961	1962	1963	1964	1965	1966	1967	1968	1969
Price Range, $	3017-3727	3102-3167								
Weight Range, lbs.	3865-3945	3760-3820								
Wheelbases, in.	122	122								
8 Cyl. Engines, hp	295-305	265								

Dodge

**Dodge Division of Chrysler Corp.
Hamtramck, Michigan**

Chrysler Corporation's second-best-selling make enjoyed steady progress and a proliferation of markets during the 1960s. Dodge entered the decade as a producer of respected but dull medium-priced automobiles, and left as one of the leading names in high performance. In product orientation, the division pushed upward into the market vacated by DeSoto, and downward into the compact and "ponycar" fields. As a result, volume increased rapidly. From 1964 through 1969, Dodge built an average of half a million cars a year. In the high-sales year of 1968, the division built a record 621,136 cars. The competition was increasing output too, so Dodge's standing in the production race varied. In its best years, the division ranked sixth; in its worst, 1961 and 1962, Dodge was ninth. The relatively poor showing in the early 1960s was temporary; Dodge quickly reorientated its product line and rapidly recovered. As Robert McCurry assumed the post of division president in the mid-1960s, Dodge achieved new status as the builder of hot performance cars.

Dodge cars had been offered on only one fairly long wheelbase in 1959. For 1960, recognizing public interest in smaller cars, Dodge added the new Dart series of sixes and V-8s, on a 118-inch wheelbase for sedans and hardtops, and a 122-inch wheelbase for wagons. Darts were available in three sub-series: Seneca, Pioneer, and Phoenix. The largest Dodges,

Matador and Polara, rode 122-inch wheelbases and were offered with V-8s only. They came in six different body styles.

Dodge's six-cylinder engine was the larger of two excellent Chrysler Corporation slant sixes. It displaced 225 cubic inches (bore and stroke 3.40 x 4.125 inches) and developed 145 bhp at 4000 rpm. This engine continued with that output in various Dodge models throughout the 1960s. The Dart V-8 was another solid and reliable unit. It displaced 318 cubic inches (bore and stroke 3.91 x 3.31), and developed either 230 hp (standard) or 255 hp (optional) in the Pioneer. The big Dodges came with larger engines. Matadors used the Chrysler 361-cid V-8 (4.12 x 3.38), which developed 295 hp; Polaras used the 383-cid V-8 (4.25 x 3.38) with 325 or 330 hp. This last engine was optional in the Matador and Phoenix.

Unit body-chassis construction was new at Dodge in 1960. It was accompanied by a complete restyling of the previous models. The Dart and the large Dodges got "chromey" front ends, large blunt grilles, and tail fins. (The fins of the big cars ended ahead of the taillights; the Dart's ran all the way back). Despite their heavy-handed styling, the cars were relatively light, and offered good performance and reasonable economy. The year brought an industry-wide recovery from the 1958-59 recession, and Dodge volume doubled.

1960 Dodge Dart Seneca Two-Door Sedan

1961 Dodge Lancer 770 Two-Door Hardtop

1960 Dodge Polara Two-Door Hardtop

1961 Dodge Dart Phoenix Four-Door Hardtop

1962 Dodge Dart 440 Four-Door Hardtop

1964 Dodge Polara 500 Two-Door Hardtop

1962 Dodge Custom 880 Four-Door Hardtop

1964 Dodge Custom 880 Convertible

1963 Dodge Dart 270 Convertible

1965 Dodge Dart GT Convertible

By 1961 Dodge was ready with its own version of the compact Valiant. Called Lancer, the small Dodge used the basic Valiant body shell and 106.5-inch wheelbase. It had a horizontal-bar grille instead of Valiant's square one, and slightly better trim. Lancers came in a 170 and a 770 series. The price of the former started at only $1,981. Each series included sedans and wagons, and the 770 also included a $2,166 hardtop. Lancer power came from a slant six of 170 cubic-inch displacement (bore and stroke 3.43 x 3.125 inches). It developed 101 horsepower. The Dart's 225-cid six was optional.

The Dart was face-lifted for 1961, with a full-width concave grille incorporating quad headlights, and reverse-slant tail fins. The six and V-8 Seneca, Pioneer, and Phoenix models continued. The large Dodge came only in the Polara series, though a convertible Dart was added to the V-8 Phoenix range. Darts and Polaras were offered again with 1960's lineup of 318 to 383 V-8s. The highest-performance power plant was the 383 cubic-inch D500 engine, which developed 330 hp. Twin four-barrel carburetors and ram-induction were responsible for this outstand-

ing horsepower, and made the Polara an extraordinarily fast automobile: It was fully capable of 120 miles an hour. Oversize Chrysler brakes and torsion-bar front suspension combined to make the D500 as roadable as it was fast. Since the ram-induction engine was available on Darts as well as Polaras, Dodge also had an extremely quick "intermediate." A D500 Dart Phoenix offered almost one horsepower for every 10 pounds of weight.

Sales dropped by over 25 percent in 1961, as a result of increased competition in the compact-car market, and an overall downward trend in the industry. Dodge's Lancer did not sell well. Introduced in 1961, Lancer was seen as a temporary entry. As developmental work on a new Dodge compact progressed, the Lancer returned for '62 with a busier grille as its only significant renovation.

New for 1962 were the brand-new body and 116-inch wheelbase of the Dart and Polara. Inspired by the designer Virgil Exner, the 1962 Dodges were as much as 400 pounds lighter and six inches shorter than the '61s. If Americans liked compacts, Exner had rea-

Dodge

soned, they'd also prefer downsized versions of standard cars. But Exner was 15 years ahead of his time. The '62s did not sell well. Most manufacturers enjoyed increased sales that year, but Dodge sales improved only slightly. Sales of the shorter models—the Dart 330 and 440, Polara and Polara 500—fell from 1961 levels. What saved the division was a separate line of Chrysler-based large cars on a 122-inch wheelbase, the 880 and Custom 880.

While Plymouth struggled on with shortened models for 1963, Dodge increased the standard wheelbase of its cars to 119 inches. Dodge also emphasized performance. A big, 413 cubic-inch V-8, which developed 360 hp, was available for 880s. The hemi-head V-8 returned as the Ramcharger engine. This 426 cubic-inch mill had aluminum pistons and high-lift cam. It developed 415 or 425 hp. Ramchargers were available for the light 330 and 440, and the Polaras. These big power plants won for Dodge the National Hot Rod Association championship in 1962. The 330 reigned supreme on literally every dragstrip. The Hemis were also strong contenders at Daytona. In 1964, Dodges and Plymouths finished 1-2-3 in the 500-mile race.

Also new for 1963 was a new compact replacement for the ailing Lancer: Dodge added five inches to the Valiant wheelbase for all models except wagons and created the all-new Dart. Hardtops, sedans, wagons, and convertibles were offered. Sales rebounded, and Dodge moved ahead of Mercury into eighth place for 1963.

The 1964 lineup was substantially the same as 1963's, distinguished only by face-lifts. Darts could be ordered with the 273-cid Valiant V-8, which developed 180 hp. The Dart GT hardtop and convertible were snazzy, and priced remarkably low at $2,300 to $2,500. The big Dodges came with the usual assortment of sixes and V-8s up to and including the Ramcharger. The 880 continued to satisfy big-car customers. Dodge climbed back into sixth place in 1963 for the first time since 1960.

The Dart got only a minor face-lift for 1965. The division revised its midrange line with new styling on a 117-inch wheelbase for all models but the wagons, which rode a 116-inch wheelbase. An old name, Coronet, was reinstated to designate this intermediate.

A special 115-inch wheelbase Coronet Hemi-Charger was offered. It was a two-door sedan that weighed just 3,165 pounds. The Hemi-Charger was perhaps one of the greatest performance bargains of the decade. It sold at a base price of $3,200. The price included heavy-duty springs and shocks, anti-roll bar,

1965 Dodge Monaco Two-Door Hardtop

1966 Dodge Charger

1965 Dodge Coronet 500 Two-Door Hardtop

1967 Dodge Dart GT Two-Door Hardtop

1966 Dodge Coronet 500 Two-Door Hardtop

1967 Dodge Monaco Four-Door Hardtop

1968 Dodge Dart GTS Two-Door Hardtop

1969 Dodge Charger

1968 Dodge Coronet 440 Two-Door Hardtop

1969 Dodge Polara 500 Two-Door Hardtop

four-speed transmission, and strong "police" brakes. The Hemi-Charger was dynamite. It could accelerate to 60 mph in seven seconds, and hit a top speed of 120 mph. In racing tune, developing up to 430 hp, it ruled the tracks in 1965.

The '65 line also included the glamorous Coronet 500 hardtop and convertible with bucket seats and center console; plus a completely new 121-inch wheelbase line of Polaras, Custom 880s and sports/luxury Monaco hardtop. Aside from the wagons, the Monaco, priced at $3,355, was the most expensive model in the lineup.

For 1966, the offering continued to be six and V-8 Darts; six and V-8 Coronets in standard, deluxe, 440 and 500 guise; V-8 Polaras and Monacos; and a hardtop Monaco 500. The Custom 880 was dropped, because Monaco sales had soared. A bright new offering was the fastback Dodge Charger, which used the 117-inch wheelbase. Although it was based on the standard Coronet body, the Charger had a look all its own: It had hidden headlamps, fold-down rear seats, and a sporty interior. Its basic engine was the 318 V-8, but the 361, 383 and 426 Hemi V-8s were available as options. So were manual transmission, "Rallye" suspension, and long list of luxury equipment. A 383 Charger with TorqueFlite automatic could run 0-60 mph in about nine seconds and hit nearly 110 mph.

Dodge restyled most of its models for 1967. Dart hardtops, sedans, and convertibles continued on the 111-inch wheelbase, but the Dart wagons were dropped. The new Darts had good-looking, clean-lined bodies. Monaco and Polara adopted the Newport's

styling and fastback-like roofline. They had a much lower profile than their predecessors and rode a 122-inch wheelbase. The Charger retained its 1966 look, but the Coronet got a face-lift. New additions to the Coronet range were the Coronet R/T (Road/Track) hardtop and convertible. Standard R/T equipment included 440-cid, 374-hp engine; heavy-duty suspension; wide tires; and oversize brakes. The 426 Hemi V-8 was again listed as an option for the Coronet R/T and the Charger.

The approach for 1968 was to face-lift the Dart, Polara, and Monaco, and to completely restyle the Coronet and Charger. These were the best-looking Dodge intermediates of the decade. They had a long, low, bullet-shaped fuselage; large windows; a plain grille; and strong but light bumpers. The Charger had hidden headlamps and a recessed rear window.

Several new model variations appeared among the 1968 compacts and intermediates. The Dart GTS series comprised plush, grand-touring hardtops and convertibles that were available with a new lightweight 340-cid V-8 that developed either 275 or 300 hp. The Coronet Super Bee was a light, fast two-door coupe, equipped with a special 335-hp version of the 383 engine. It sold for only $3,027. R/T equipment was made available for the Charger as well as the Coronet. This resulted in a fine road car.

The Super Bee, Dart GTS, Coronet and Charger R/Ts composed what Dodge called its "Scat Pack." They were denoted by bumble-bee stripes. These high-performance cars were among the most roadable machines anyone could buy in America during 1968.

1969 Dodge Charger Daytona

Dodge

The R/T's ultimate engines, a 375-hp Magnum 440 and a 425-hp Hemi, made it a winning entry on the nation's drag strips once again.

Like all the Chrysler models, with which they shared bodies, the Polara and Monaco received all-new "fuselage" styling for 1969, but retained their 122-inch wheelbase. The Dart, Coronet and Charger were face-lifted. Chargers got a new split grille; Coronet R/Ts and 500s sported full-width taillamp assemblies. The usual wide range of engines was offered: 170-cid and 240-cid sixes for Darts and Coronets; 273,318 and 383 V-8s for Darts, Coronets, Chargers and Polaras; 383 V-8s for Monacos, Polaras, Chargers, and Coronets; a Magnum 335-hp version for the Coronet Super Bee; and 440 V-8s for the Monaco and Polara wagons. A 375-hp Magnum 440 was standard for the Charger and Coronet R/Ts, and was optional on all Polaras and Monacos except wagons. The 426 Hemi was available as an option on R/T models. A new variation was the Dart Swinger hardtop coupe. It had special identifying trim, and a bright aluminum grille. A choice of 318- or 340-cid V-8s was available for the Swinger.

The pride of the '69 fleet was the exotic Charger Daytona, a specialty car built especially for the Daytona 500. The Daytona had a wind-cheating nose, a front spoiler, an aerodynamic rear window, and a huge rear deck stabilizer. Compared with the previous Charger 500 racing car, the Daytona was about 20 percent more aerodynamic. This gave the new car an advantage of 500 yards per lap. Dodge built only 505 Charger Daytonas, just enough to qualify them as production cars for NASCAR racing. The list price was about $3,900. A Daytona won at the Talledega 500 in September 1969; arch-rival Ford failed to show up. In 1970, the Daytonas and Plymouth's similar Superbird won 38 of 48 major NASCAR races.

It had been a great decade for Dodge.

DODGE AT A GLANCE, 1960-1969										
	1960	1961	1962	1963	1964	1965	1966	1967	1968	1969
Price Range, $	2278-3621	1979-3409	1951-3407	1983-3407	1988-3420	2074-3527	2094-3604	2224-3712	2323-3869	2400-4046
Weight Range, lbs.	3385-4220	2585-4125	2495-4055	2605-4186	2615-4185	2645-4355	2665-4315	2710-4475	2705-4360	2711-4361
Wheelbases, in.	118-122	106.5-122	106.5-122	106-122	106-122	106-121	106-121	111-122	111-122	111-122
6 Cyl. Engines, hp	145	101-145	101-145	101-145	101-145	101-145	101-145	115-145	115-145	101-145
8 Cyl. Engines, hp	230-330	230-330	230-305	230-425	180-425	180-425	180-425	180-425	190-425	190-425

Edsel

**Edsel Division of Ford Motor Co.
Dearborn, Michigan**

In 1960 Ford's Edsel concluded three years of consistent failure. Ford started in 1958 with a production goal of 100,000 Edsels a year, but barely managed to produce that many cars over three model years. The total for the final year was 2,846 units.

The Edsel was condemned by inaccurate product planning. When it was being developed in 1955, the low to medium price field was wide open. Pontiac, Buick, and Dodge were producing nearly two million vehicles for this market. The Edsel was intended to fill what appeared to be a gap in the market between Ford and Mercury. In a way, it was the missing model that Ford had planned but not produced in 1949, when the intended lineup had been Ford, Mercury, Lincoln, and Zephyr.

Unfortunately, the Edsel marque didn't appear until 1958, the worst possible year for any new offering. By then, the middle-price market had slumped drastically. By mid-1959, there was no market for the Edsel. The 1960 models, which bore a close resemblance to concurrent Fords, were withdrawn soon after they were announced in October 1959.

The 1958 line of Edsels had included Ranger, Corsair, Pacer, Citation, and station wagon models. In 1959, the Pacer and Citation were dropped; in 1960 the Corsair disappeared. Only seven 1960 models were offered. These were Ranger two-door and four-door sedans, a hardtop coupe, a hardtop sedan, and a convertible; and Villager wagons with nine-passenger or six-passenger capacity. Rangers were offered with standard or deluxe trim, except for the convertible, which came only in deluxe form.

The 1960 Edsel's standard engine was a 292 cubic-inch V-8, which developed 185 horsepower. At no extra cost, a buyer could order Ford's 223 cubic-inch in-line six, which provided 145 hp. For $58 more, the customer could have the "Super Express" V-8, which displaced 352 cubic inches and developed 300

1960 Edsel Ranger Convertible

1960 Edsel Ranger Four-Door Sedan

hp. Super Express V-8s were fast, capable of 0-60 mph times of less than 10 seconds.

For 1960, the upright central grille was replaced by a Ford-like horizontal motif that was divided in the center. Heavy chrome accents were used on the fenders and sides of the body. Two-speed or three-speed automatic transmission, power steering and air conditioning were options. The Ranger convertible, equipped with air conditioning, and other options, could run up to $3,800.

Extremely low production makes the 1960 Edsel the rarest of the marque's three model years. Only 76 convertibles were made. There were 135 hardtop sedans, 295 hardtop coupes, 777 two-door sedans, 1,288 four-door sedans, and 275 station wagons.

	EDSEL AT A GLANCE, 1960-1969									
	1960	**1961**	**1962**	**1963**	**1964**	**1965**	**1966**	**1967**	**1968**	**1969**
Price Range, $	2643-3072									
Weight Range, lbs.	3601-4046									
Wheelbases, in.	120									
6 Cyl. Engines, hp	145									
8 Cyl. Engines, hp	185-300									

Excalibur

SS Automobiles Inc.
Milwaukee, Wisconsin

America's most successful builder of cars fashioned in the image of classic forebears is Excalibur, the Milwaukee concern founded by the industrial designer Brooks Stevens. The cars are assembled fastidiously; and they're superb road machines. There have never been enough of them to meet demand. The company's output has always been miniscule. Stevens often calls Excalibur "America's number five auto producer." Checker produces far more cars than Excalibur does, but Stevens says he doesn't think of Checkers as automobiles—taxicabs, maybe.

The Excalibur Series I, introduced in 1964, remained in its original form until it was replaced by the Series II in 1970. Its styling overtones were those of the classic 1928 Mercedes-Benz SSK. Even Excalibur's sales literature was patterned after that of the prewar Mercedes. Careful engineering and clever design distinguished the Excalibur from the motley group of VW-powered replicas that followed it.

In 1964, Stevens was finishing four years of design consulting for the ill-fated Studebaker Corporation. Studebaker had ceased car production at its South Bend, Indiana, plant in late 1963, but continued some operations at its Hamilton, Ontario, factory. Stevens hoped that Studebaker's production would go on. He was unimpressed by Studebaker's showing of mundane cars at the 1964 Chicago Auto Show, and was determined to build a Studebaker "special" for the New York show in April. Stevens ordered a Lark Daytona convertible chassis with power disc brakes, and a

290-horsepower, supercharged 289-cid Avanti V-8. Studebaker managers tentatively approved his plan to build "a modern classic" for their company's New York display.

The prototype Excalibur was created in just six weeks by Stevens and his two sons, David and William. No sooner had it left for New York than Studebaker officials changed their minds. A "contemporary classic," they said, would conflict with the image of the "common sense car."

More than time and money was at stake for Stevens. He refused to scrap the project. Through hurried phone calls to the management of the New York show, he arranged to display the Excalibur separately from the Studebakers. The car was a hit. In August 1964, Stevens and his sons founded SS Automobiles to manufacture it. One hundred copies of the car had been sold by the beginning of 1966.

The demise of Studebaker ended the supply of the 289 V-8s after 1965, so Stevens went shopping for a new engine. The new V-8, a 327-cid Corvette engine, was provided by Stevens's friends Ed Cole and Semon E. "Bunkie" Knudson at General Motors. It pumped out 300 horsepower in standard tune. After 1966, Excaliburs were also offered with a Paxton-supercharged V-8, which was rated at 400 horsepower, and high-performance Corvette engines. Using the standard 3.31:1 rear axle ratio, Stevens claimed his car was capable of a 0 to 60 time of less than five seconds and a top speed in the area of 160 mph. This was a

1967-69 Excalibur Series I Phaeton

CONSUMER GUIDE®

considerable improvement over the 289, which did 0 to 60 in about seven seconds.

The 109-inch wheelbase Studebaker Daytona convertible chassis was hardly modern, but it offered some advantages. Unlike concurrent torque-box frames, it was quite narrow, since its frame rails were not built far out to accommodate more modern body sills. As a convertible chassis it was firmly X-braced. But considerable chassis engineering was needed to insure safe handling from a high-powered car that was at least 500 pounds lighter than a Corvette.

David Stevens was largely responsible for the Excalibur's engineering. The car's classic-style cowl forced him to lower the Studebaker steering column and control pedals. And that was just the beginning of the changes required. It was necessary to drastically alter the suspension geometry by decreasing the spring rates and changing the caster and camber. Like all Excaliburs that followed, the 1965-69 Series I was fast both on curves and straights. The modified Studebaker chassis was retained for all Series I cars. (For the 1970 Series II David Stevens designed his own box-section frame with four-wheel independent suspension.)

Brooks Stevens was responsible for the styling, which was a surprisingly accurate rendition of the old SSK. To Stevens, outside exhaust pipes were mandatory, but no one in the United States could supply them. Ultimately, Stevens bought the flexible pipe from the same German firm that had supplied it to Mercedes-Benz back in the 1920s. The bodies of the first few cars were made of hammered aluminum; SS soon switched to fiberglass for reasons of cost and practicality. The radiator was made of sheet brass for the prototype; production radiators were cast alumninum. Mercedes-Benz suggested the hood emblem, an Excalibur sword in a circle. This resembled but did not compromise Mercedes's three-pointed star, of which the German firm is notoriously protective. French-built free-standing headlamps closely resembled those of the original SSK units. White-on-black instruments from the Studebaker Hawk were placed in an SSK-like engine-turned dashboard panel. The seats used were modified Studebaker buckets, upholstered in expanded vinyl. (Later, leather would be used.) The initial price was almost unbelievable: $7,250, for a hand-built

car having one of the most competently engineered chassis in the business.

For 1966, SS Automobiles expanded its line by adding a more elaborate roadster. Unlike the aggressive-looking SSK, the roadster had complete fenders and running boards. By 1967, the line also included a phaeton, which offered seating for four and an easy-to-use convertible top. The SS phaeton was surprisingly roomy. Stevens happily pointed out that its headroom was within an inch of the Cadillac Eldorado's, and its legroom exceeded that of the Cadillac. And an Excalibur phaeton had twice as many seats as a Corvette.

The price rose, but the cars remained remarkable bargains. Base price was about $10,000 by 1969. It wasn't until inflation and government-mandated emissions controls and safety equipment of the 1970s took their toll that Excaliburs became $20,000-plus automobiles.

As prices went up, the equipment offered and materials used increased in variety and quality. Standard equipment by 1969 included air conditioning, heater and defroster, variable-ratio power steering, tilt-type steering wheel, power disc front brakes, positraction rear axle, chrome-plated wire wheels, luggage rack, AM-FM stereo, leather seats, Turbo-Hydra-matic transmission, twin side-mounted spare tires, all-weather hardtop, air horns, driving lights, steel-belted radial ply tires, and automatically controlled self-leveling rear shock absorbers.

Excaliburs are still being built today, as the Series III. They have a 454-cid Corvette engine and elaborate styling. The Series III updated the Series I and II from circa 1928 to 1933, and will continue in production until around 1982. By then or before then, the Series IV will be introduced. We assume that it will update the line still further.

The lithe cycle-fendered SSK model is the definitive Excalibur, and the model most sought after by collectors. It has not been built since the '60s, but it will not be forgotten. In it Brooks Stevens realized his dream of a contemporary classic. He likes to quote Mercedes-Benz's 1928 brochure: "You looked, you ran your hand over the pristinely white lacquered fenders, you sat on the lush black leather, you drove. Then you either bought it or inwardly wept."

EXCALIBUR AT A GLANCE, 1960-1969										
	1960	1961	1962	1963	1964	1965	1966	1967	1968	1969
Price Range, $						7250-8000	7250-8000	8000-9000	9000-9500	10,000-11,000
Weight Range, lbs.						2100	2100-2500	2300-2500	2300-2600	2400-2650
Wheelbases, in.						109	109	109	109	109
8 Cyl. Engines, hp						290	300-400	300-435	300-435	300-435

Ford
Ford Motor Co.
Dearborn, Michigan

The history of Ford in the 1960s closely parallels that of Chevrolet, its arch-rival. When the decade ended, Ford was producing only about 100,000 more cars a year as when the '60s began. During this period, the company expanded into several important new markets. These areas developed because the public desired sportier or more economical forms of transportation. And like Chevrolet, Ford built these diverse models on relatively few wheelbases. (The two most specialized Fords, Mustang and Thunderbird, are discussed elsewhere.)

Ford management changed rapidly during the 1960s. The decade began with the arrival of Lee A. Iacocca as the division's general manager in 1960. In 1961, George Walker left as chief stylist, and Eugene Bordinat became Ford's chief of automotive design. Iacocca soon put an end to Robert S. MacNamara's concept of building mundane people-haulers. By the end of the decade, Ford was offering some of the world's best road cars. Throughout the '60s, Fords were the cars to beat on the nation's racetracks. In fact, the 1968-69 Dodge Charger racing program was designed to finally beat the super-stockers from Ford. In this period, Ford also evolved from a "Chevy-follower" to a "Chevy-leader." Its compact Falcon outsold the Corvair; its 1962 Fairlane intermediate was a year ahead of, and more popular than, the Chevy II; its Mustang changed the public's attitude toward compact cars and sent Chevrolet to the drawing boards to develop the Camaro.

Looking at Ford in terms of the size of its products is probably the best way to summarize its cars. The smallest was the Falcon, which rode a 109.5-inch wheelbase through 1965 and a wheelbase of 111-inches (113 inches for wagons) from 1966 on. Falcon production gradually decreased, largely because of competition from both inside and outside Ford Division. But the car was always a profit-maker. To many, it was the ultimate "throw-away" car: It was built to sell at a very low price, and was designed to be discarded within five years. (Some said one year). Compared with the Corvair, Falcon's conventional independent front suspension, beam-axle rear suspension, and ordinary 170 cubic-inch six-cylinder engine were uninteresting, but they combined to make a simple little car that rode well, stopped well, provided excellent space utilization, and delivered 20 to 25 miles per gallon. What's more, the Falcon could be serviced by back-yard mechanics; a similar claim could not be made for the Corvair.

Ford brought out the bucket-seated Falcon Futura coupe, its answer to the Corvair Monza, in the spring of 1961. This was a sporty little car that was restyled in 1964 to a much less distinctive, squared-off shape. The "ultimate" collector's Falcon, however, is the

1960 Ford Falcon Two-Door Sedan

1961 Ford Galaxie Two-Door Sedan

1961 Ford Galaxie Sunliner Convertible

1962 Ford Galaxie Two-Door Sedan

1963 Ford Fairlane 500 Four-Door Sedan

Futura Sprint, which was introduced in 1963½. Offered as a convertible or hardtop, it was powered by a compact yet lively 260 cubic-inch Fairlane V-8. This was one of the finest engines built, and one of the most economical. The 260 completely transformed Falcon performance without greatly affecting gas mileage. Sprints had special trim, bucket seats, console, and special instruments, including a 6000-rpm tachometer. When equipped with optional four-speed transmission, they were spritely cars that were fun to drive.

In 1966, the Falcon was restyled a third time. It received a longer wheelbase and a long-hood, short-deck body that was reminiscent of the Mustang. The Falcon remained in this form through the rest of the '60s. When Ford increased the 260 cubic-inch V-8 to 289 cubic inches, this engine also became a Falcon option. In its last year before emission controls, the 289 "Stage 2" engine offered 225 horsepower with four-barrel carburetors, and made Falcon Sprints very fast. For 1968, the 289 engine was detuned to 195 hp, but Ford made the larger 302-cid V-8 available as an option for Falcons. Equipped with a two-barrel carburetor, the 302 ran on regular gas and developed 210 hp. With the four-barrel, it required premium fuel, but developed 230 hp. Stringent emission controls forced Ford to drop the four-barrel package by 1969.

In 1962, Ford broke new ground with the "intermedi-ate-sized" Fairlane. The name (originally derived from Henry Ford's estate) had been lifted from the large Ford line. In concept, the Fairlane was identical with Virgil Exner's downsized 1962 Plymouths and Dodges. Unlike Plymouth and Dodge, however, Ford retained its full-sized cars. That was a wise move, because the Fairlane sold only about 79,600 units for 1962, and didn't break the 100,000-unit level until 1968.

The Fairlane was a significant car for reasons other than sales volume. It was the first Ford to use the 260 cubic-inch small-block V-8, the basis of some of Ford's hottest performance models. Bored out to 289 cubic inches in 1963 as an option, this engine developed 271 hp, almost one horsepower per cubic inch. Stroked to 302 cid in 1968, it delivered 230 hp when equipped with the optional carburetor. Powerful and smooth, yet surprisingly economical, this engine in all three displacement configurations was the definitive small-block V-8. Tuned versions, in racing cars and sports cars like the Ford GT40 and Cobra, disproved the old saw about there being no substitute for cubic inches. The GT40 nearly took the world GT Manufacturers Trophy away from Ferrari in 1964, its first full year of competition. In 1966 and 1967, it won the LeMans 24 Hours.

The Fairlane rode a 115.5-inch wheelbase in its first forms. It came came only as a two-door or four-door

1962 Ford Falcon Futura Two-Door Coupe

1964 Ford Falcon Two-Door Sedan

1963 Ford Galaxie 500 Two-Door Hardtop

1965 Ford Galaxie 500 LTD Four-Door Hardtop

1963 Ford Falcon Futura Sprint Two-Door Hardtop

1966 Ford Country Squire Station Wagon

Ford

sedan during 1962. As time went on, Fairlanes became more exciting. Along with a number of station wagons, a new line of Fairlane 500s were added in 1963. A bucket-seated 500 hardtop with an engine that developed up to 271 hp sold for $2,500. Some of the best Fairlanes appeared in 1966. The body was completely restyled and mounted on a 116-inch wheelbase (113 inches for wagons). These were long, sleek cars with smooth lines. They had curved side glass and vertical taillights. The 1966 top-of-the-line models were the 500XL hardtop coupe and convertible. Although they could be ordered with Ford's 120-hp six, most were equipped with the 289 cubic-inch, 200-hp V-8. The fastest models were the 500XL GTs, which had as standard equipment a new 390 cubic-inch engine. Rated at 335 horsepower, this potent power plant had 10.5:1 compression and used premium fuel. Since the 390 could be ordered with any Fairlane, racing drivers used them in the lighter two-door sedans that were respected for their competitive prowess. From 1964 on, Ford offered a growing assortment of Fairlane handling and performance options, including stiff suspension and four-speed gearboxes.

In 1968, the Fairlanes were again restyled. The Torino was introduced as a top-of-the-line Fairlane subseries. Torinos were available with the 115-hp six. The GTs were the most exciting models. Instead of the normal Torino lineup of sedan, hardtop, and wagon, GTs came as hardtop coupes, convertibles, and sleek fastbacks. GTs featured bucket seats, center console, paint striping, and more performance options than a Ford salesman could memorize. Standard was the 302 cubic-inch V-8, which developed 210 hp, but a buyer could order a GT with the big Ford 427 cubic-inch V-8, which developed 390 hp from its 10.9:1 compression and four-barrel carburetors.

For 1969, the same Torino packages were offered again, with one important addition: the fastback and hardtop Torino Cobra. The name symbolized Ford's close relationship with Carroll Shelby's muscle-bound

sports cars. The Torino Cobra came with the 428 cubic-inch Mach I engine, which provided 335 hp. This power plant had first appeared in the 1968½ Mercury Cyclone, and was known as the Cobra Jet. A $133 option was "Ram-Air," a fiberglass hood scoop and special air cleaner assembly that ducted incoming air directly into the carburetor through a valve in the air cleaner.

Torino Cobras came with four-speed gearbox, competition suspension, which included stiff shocks and springs, and functional hood locking pins. One magazine was actually disappointed when its Torino Cobra ran from 0 to 60 in 7.2 seconds and the quarter mile in 15 seconds at 98.3 miles per hour! On the other hand, just about everyone admitted that of all the 1969 "supercars"—Plymouth GTX, Dodge Charger R/T, Pontiac GTO, Chevelle 396, and Buick GS 400—the Torino Cobra was the tightest, the best built, and the quietest.

The Torinos were potent racing machines. Ford found that the Torino GT-based Mercury Cyclone was slightly more aerodynamic than other Torinos, and began using only Cyclones in races more than 250 miles long in 1969. Nevertheless, both the Torino and the Cyclone could achieve about 190 mph. Lee Roy Yarborough won the 1969 Daytona 500 in a Ford.

Despite Falcon and Fairlane developments, Ford was still a determined producer of full-size automobiles in the 1960s. The big models—the Custom, pre-1962 Fairlane, Galaxie, Galaxie 500, 500XL, and LTD—all used Ford's 119-inch wheelbase (it increased to 121 inches in 1969). They were all heavy cars, and not particularly exciting to drive on anything other than a superhighway. But plenty of interesting variations developed that made these 3,000-pound to 4,000-pound monsters surprisingly capable, even on winding roads.

The big-car lineup of 1960 Custom, Fairlane, Galaxie, and station wagon came with sixes and V-8s. All had been hastily restyled to keep pace with the incredibly finned 1959 Chevrolet. But to everyone's surprise, the boxy 1959 Fords had outsold the Chevys. So in 1961, Ford again gave its cars a face-lifting, clipped their fins, and reverted to a full-width grille similar to that of the 1959 Galaxie and round taillights. The bucket-seated Galaxie 500XL Victoria hardtop coupe and Sunliner convertible appeared in 1962½. The latter, priced at $3,518, was the most expensive car in Ford's lineup. The "500" stood for the 500-mile races in which Fords were doing well. (In 1963, Ford won every 500 race!) Although the standard power train was a 292 cubic-inch V-8 and Cruise-O-Matic, a large number of options could be ordered to turn a 500XL into a fire-breather. There were 300-hp, 340-hp, and 401-hp versions of the 390-cid V-8, plus a Borg Warner four-speed gearbox. In 1963, an even larger engine was added. It boasted 406 cubic inches and up to 405 horsepower. But this engine was rarely ordered for "street Fords," even 500XLs.

The large 1963 models were face-lifted, and augmented midyear with a new set of Galaxie 500 and

1967 Ford Galaxie 500/XL Two-Door Hardtop

1968 Ford Falcon Futura Station Wagon

1969 Ford Falcon Futura Sports Coupe

1968 Ford Galaxie 500 Convertible

1969 Ford Torino GT Two-Door Fastback

500XL sports hardtops. These cars had ultrathin fastback rooflines. Both were available with 427 cubic-inch engines. For 1964, the big cars had more sculptured sheet metal and a horizontal-bar grille, as well as a new roofline for four-door hardtop models.

The 1964 Ford lineup collectively won *Motor Trend* magazine's "Car of the Year" award on the basis of its "total performance" image. Performance was just what the big Fords delivered. A pair of Galaxie 500XLs tested by the magazine that year were truly impressive machines. The 390 V-8 powered one of them from 0 to 60 mph in 9.3 seconds; the 427 made that run in 7.4 seconds. The only complaint was the car's tendency to take a nose-dive when making quick stops, and a slight toughness in the power brakes.

The 1965 Fords were completely restyled with longer, sleeker lines. They were also fitted with a new, sophisticated front suspension. Among the new models were the Galaxie LTD hardtop coupe and sedan, priced about $3,300. LTDs were favorably compared in quietness at speed to Rolls-Royces.

Ford held its basic 1965 styling for the 1966 and 1967 models and kept the 119-inch wheelbase. The range consisted of LTD, XL, Galaxie, and Custom models, with sixes and V-8s from 150 to 340 hp. The 1968 models had new sheet metal below the beltline, and concealed headlights for XL and LTD models. The 1969 cars had new sheet metal everywhere and a wheelbase that was two inches longer, a tunneled backlight for SportsRoof (fastback) models, and ventless front door glass on hardtops and convertibles. The LTD, which had become a separate model in 1967, had increased its strength in the marketplace. Ford built nearly 139,000 LTDs in the 1968 model year, and more than twice that many in 1969. Ford also made more than 339,000 Galaxie 500s, about 62,000 500XLs, and some 114,000 Customs for 1969.

Throughout the decade, Ford production kept pace with Chevrolet's, often coming close to leading. In 1965, Ford enjoyed its first two-million-car year, and by 1970, it was number one in output, producing over 140,000 more cars than its rival.

FORD AT A GLANCE, 1960-1969										
	1960	**1961**	**1962**	**1963**	**1964**	**1965**	**1966**	**1967**	**1968**	**1969**
Price Range, $	1912-3080	1912-3127	1985-3518	1985-3518	1996-3495	2020-3498	2060-3872	2118-3493	2252-3619	2283-3738
Weight Range, lbs.	2259-4122	2254-4064	2243-4078	2300-4000	2365-4000	2366-3959	2519-4062	2520-4049	2680-4059	2700-4227
Wheelbases, in.	109.5-119	109.5-119	109.5-119	109.5-119	109.5-119	109.5-119	111-119	111-119	111-119	111-121
6 Cyl. Engines, hp	90-145	85-135	85-138	85-138	85-138	105-150	105-150	105-150	100-150	100-155
8 Cyl. Engines, hp	185-300	175-300	164-401	145-425	164-425	200-425	200-425	200-425	195-390	220-360

Ford Mustang
Ford Division of Ford Motor Co.
Dearborn, Michigan

The greatest single automotive success of the 1960s raised Ford volume by well over half a million cars, and set an all-time record for first-year sales of any new model. Between its introduction date in April 1964 and January 1965, a total of 680,989 copies of the Mustang were sold. Truck drivers drove through showroom windows staring at them, housewives entered contests to win them, and dealers auctioned them off because buyer demand exceeded supply by 15 to 1. America loved the Mustang.

This remarkable accomplishment can be credited to Lee A. Iacocca, the engineer-turned-salesman who worked his way from an obscure sales position to vice-president and general manager of Ford Division in five years. Iacocca later became president of Ford Motor Company (and recently was named president of Chrysler Corporation).

Iacocca's idea was a new "personal car." In his early days as sales manager, people had pleaded with him to bring back the two-seat Thunderbird. Iacocca dreamed, doodled, and scribbled down thoughts in the little black book by which he governed his career. By 1961 he had developed a plan. His young-person's car would be inexpensive to build, but peppy and sporty-looking. It would sell for less than $2,500. He projected a volume of 100,000 units a year.

The first Mustang prototype was a low, fiberglass two-seater on a 90-inch wheelbase, powered by a Ford Cardinal (soon to become the German Ford Taunus 12M) two-liter V-4 that developed 90 horsepower. This Mustang I was pretty but impractical. When Iacocca looked at the people who gathered around it at a show,

he said: "That's sure not the car we want to build, because it can't be a volume car. It's too far out." More prototypes followed, culminating in the four-seat, conventionally powered, 108-inch-wheelbase production Mustang of 1964½. From a marketing standpoint, it could not have been much better.

From 1965 through the 1968 model year the Mustang came in three basic forms: a hardtop, a convertible, and a semi-fastback coupe. Convertible sales started at the 100,000-unit annual level but had dropped to less than 15,000 a year by 1969. The crisp notchback hardtop was the sales leader. The coupe, known as the "2+2," was introduced with the rest of the Ford line in autumn 1964. It soon overtook the convertible in sales and averaged about 50,000 units a year through 1969.

The standard Mustang engines during the first six months of production were the 170 cubic-inch Falcon six that developed 101 hp, and the 260-cid smallblock V-8 that provided 164 hp. By fall, these had been replaced by Ford's 200-cid six that was rated at 120 hp, and the bored-out 289 V-8 that developed 200 hp (or 271 hp with four-barrel carburetor). In the last years of the 1960s, before the federal government put an end to Ford's "Total Performance" program, the company offered increasingly hairy engine options for the Mustang. For 1967, the cars could be ordered with a 390 V-8 that developed 320 hp; for 1968, the most powerful engine was a 427 that provided 390 hp; for 1969, a 335-hp 428 was available.

Mustang's appeal lay in its myriad options, which enabled a customer to personalize the car. Careful use

Mustang II Prototype

1965 Mustang Convertible

1965 Mustang GT 2+2

1966 Mustang Two-Door Hardtop

of the option order book could result in anything from a cute economy car to a thunderingly fast drag racer or a deceptively nimble sporty car. Transmission choices comprised automatics, four-speeds, three-speeds, and stick-overdrive units. Handling packages, power steering, disc brakes, air conditioning, a tachometer, and a clock were available. A Mustang could be ordered without a center console and with bench seats instead of buckets, though few people asked for this option. The Mustang GT package was a pleasant assortment of goodies priced at $170, which included disc front brakes, a full-gauge instrument panel, and special badges. A variety of interiors was available, along with accent stripes and special moldings for the exterior.

Mustang's shape was pleasant. It had been created by Joe Oros, L. David Ash, and Gayle L. Halderman of the Ford Division styling studio. The long hood and short deck style, which was to fascinate so many buyers in the 1960s and early '70s, was born with the Mustang. For the next several years, it was the only formula for what soon became known, in honor of Iacocca's wonder, as the "ponycar." Mustang styling was so good that it was hardly changed at all during the first few years. The '66s were mostly unaltered; the '67s had a deepened grille and sculptured side panels that ended in twin air scoops; the '68s had a new grille with an inner bright ring around the Mustang emblem, and simulated side air scoops. Only in 1969 was the package finally changed more extensively. The '69 Mustang was lower, longer and wider than earlier versions, and had ventless side glass, an egg-crate grille, and a "SportsRoof" fastback with simulated air scoops and rear deck spoiler. The line expanded in '69. The new models were the six or V-8 Grande hardtop coupe priced at $2,866 to $2,971, and the Mach I fastback priced at $3,139. The Mach I had a 351-cid, 250-hp V-8 as standard equipment.

Today, the Mustangs collected by enthusiasts are the 1965-68 models—especially the sporty ones with deluxe interiors, Rally Pacs, handling options, four-speeds and that gem of a V-8 engine, the 289. Their popularity is not hard to understand. They provide the fun of a sports car, room for four, and good looks.

1967 Mustang GTA 2+2

1968 Mustang Convertible

1969 Mustang Mach I

Don't let Mustang's plebian Falcon heritage fool you. Racing driver Dan Gurney, remarking about the 271-hp four-speed fastback, wrote: "This car will run the rubber off a Triumph or an MG. It has the feel of a 2+2 Ferrari. So what *is* a sports car?"

MUSTANG AT A GLANCE, 1960-1969

	1960	1961	1962	1963	1964	1965	1966	1967	1968	1969
Price Range, $						2368-2722	2416-2653	2461-2698	2602-2814	2635-3139
Weight Range, lbs.						2445-2904	2488-2650	2578-2738	2635-2745	2690-3175
Wheelbases, in.						108	108	108	108	108
6 Cyl. Engines, hp						101-120	120	120	115	115-155
8 Cyl. Engines, hp						164-271	200-271	200-320	195-390	220-335

Ford Thunderbird

Ford Division of Ford Motor Co.
Dearborn, Michigan

Ford's decision to turn its two-seat Thunderbird into a four-seat luxury car for 1958 could hardly be faulted from a marketing standpoint. In developing the 1958-60 "Squarebird," Ford created the first "personal luxury" car. And by 1960, the division was selling almost five times as many Thunderbirds a year as it had sold in 1957, the highest-volume year for the two-seater.

The 1960 Thunderbird was the last model in the three-year styling generation of squared-off four-seaters. It was substantially the same as its predecessor, but had a new grille with a main horizontal bar bisecting three vertical bars ahead of a grid insert, new triple taillight clusters, and small trim changes. As in 1958-59, the 1960 car rode a 113-inch wheelbase. A 352 cubic-inch, 300-horsepower V-8 was standard. The Lincoln Continental 430 cubic-inch V-8, which developed 350 hp at 4600 rpm, was optional. Prices averaged about $4,000. Hardtops and convertibles were offered. Hardtops outsold convertibles by nearly a seven to one ratio, indicating that T-bird customers wanted luxury first and sportiness second.

The 1961 Thunderbird was entirely new, though the 113-inch wheelbase was retained. Its styling and engineering governed the shape and image of Thunderbirds through the 1963 model year. These cars were bullet-shaped and had severely pointed front profiles, modest tail fins, and traditional circular Ford taillights. For 1961, only one engine was offered: the 390 cid V-8 (created by stroking the old 352 a quarter inch), which developed 300 hp. In 1962, the 390 engine was offered with a power package option, which increased horsepower to 340. With minor horsepower alterations, these two 390s were the standard Thunderbird power plants through 1968. They were, however, accompanied by big-block engine options in 1967-68.

Thunderbird engineering in the early and middle 1960s was conservative, but sound. Ford had considered a front-wheel-drive T-bird for 1961, but such a car was far too unorthodox to reach production. Instead, engineers stressed quality control and solid construction, high ride standards, and minimum noise at speed. Extensive use of rubber bushings in the independent front suspension and rear leaf springs made the 1961-63 Thunderbirds some of the best-riding cars of the day.

Styling for 1962 and 1963 was generally the same as that for 1961, but two new models were added. These were the Sports Roadster and the Landau.

The Sports Roadster was the only production car to go from a four-seat model to a two-seater. (There are many examples of the opposite, including the 1958 Thunderbird.) The decision was made by Lee A. Iacocca, Ford Division general manager, because dealers were beseiged with requests for another

1960 Thunderbird Two-Door Hardtop

1962 Thunderbird Convertible

1961 Thunderbird Two-Door Hardtop

1963 Thunderbird Sports Roadster

two-seater. Iacocca concluded that there was no significant market for anything like the 1955-57 Thunderbirds, but that a semi-sports model wouldn't hurt.

The designer most responsible for the Sports Roadster was Bud Kaufman, who developed a fiberglass tonneau cover, which hid the area behind the car's front seat and formed twin front-seat headrests. Kaufman overcame fitting problems so the car's soft top could operate with the cover in place. Kelsey-Hayes wire wheels were fitted to all Sports Roadsters. The stock rear fender skirts were left off because the pseudo knock-off hub caps would not clear them.

Limited demand made the Sports Roadster rare. Only 1,427 were built for 1962, and just 455 for 1963. The problem was price. The Sports Roadster sold for about $650 more than the standard Thunderbird convertible. (In 1964, dealers offered the tonneau cover and wire wheels as accessories.)

The Thunderbird Landau was more popular, because it cost only $77 more than the standard hardtop. The Landau sported a vinyl-covered roof that had a fake landau, or "S" bar, on the rear pillar. This added a distinctive touch and Landaus rapidly became popular. By 1966, they were outselling the unadorned Thunderbird hardtops, and by 1969, they composed the bulk of T-bird production.

The 1963 model run also included 2,000 Limited Edition Landaus, which had been introduced in the spring of the year. These were identified by special plaques numbered from 1 to 2,000 on the console panel. These models featured all-white backgrounds in the rear roof quarter, all-white interiors, and knock-off-style spinner wheel covers.

The Thunderbird got completely new sheet metal in 1964, along with a lot of body side sculpture. The new body style, still on the 113-inch wheelbase, remained through 1966. These were years of increasing emphasis on quiet, refined luxury. During this period, sales of Thunderbird convertibles declined noticeably. The last convertibles were run off for the 1966 model year, and they accounted for only 5,049 out of some 69,000 Thunderbirds.

Among features introduced during this fourth styling generation were a cockpit-style driver's compartment and Silent-Flo ventilation (1964); front disc brakes (1965); full-width taillight housing, including back-up lights and sequential turn signals; and a "Town" roofline on the Landau and hardtop (1966). A popular accessory, which had first appeared in 1961, was the Thunderbird's "Swing-Away" steering wheel. It shifted about 10 inches inboard so the driver could be seated more easily.

Throughout the '60s, the pros and cons of offering a Thunderbird sedan were steadily debated by Ford officials. By 1965, Iacocca was satisfied that the sporting image was being handled by other Fords: He had his new Mustang, plus an attractive array of Falcons and Fairlanes. Market surveys indicated that the Thunderbird, firmly entrenched as a personal luxury car, no longer needed the image of sportiness. Accordingly, the car was completely restyled for 1967. The convertible model was dropped, and in its place came a four-door Landau on a 117-inch wheelbase. The hardtop and two-door Landau were continued, but on a wheelbase that was two inches shorter than the four-door's. The front styling featured a deeply recessed honeycomb grille, which concealed the headlamps. The front bumper was wrapped underneath. On

1964 Thunderbird Convertible

1965 Thunderbird Convertible

1964 Thunderbird Landau

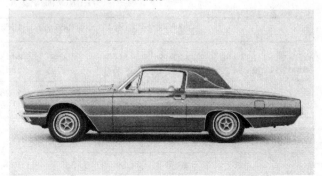

1966 Thunderbird Town Landau

Ford Thunderbird

two-door models, rear quarter windows retracted horizontally into roof pillars.

These models were sold through 1969, despite the fact that the plain Thunderbird hardtop was a slow seller, as were the other Thunderbirds in the line. Sales moved slowly but consistently downward in the last three years of the decade. The four-door Landau was not very impressive; the car's rear doors seemed to detract from its formal roofline. Sales of the four-door dropped from almost 25,000 cars in 1967 to slightly less than 16,000 for 1969.

Styling changes to distinguish the 1968 and 1969

Thunderbirds were minor. For 1968, an egg-crate grille pattern replaced the honeycomb of the 1967 model, and the body sill moldings were narrowed. For 1969, the grille texture was changed to horizontal louvers with three vertical dividers, and divided taillamps replaced the full-width cluster. The rear quarter windows of Landau coupes were eliminated.

Although the Thunderbird had no performance image to uphold in the late '60s, the Ford slogan was "Total Performance." Big-block V-8s were offered on the T-bird, but they did not sell well. The 1967 big-block option was Ford's 428 cubic-inch power plant with 345 horsepower. For 1969, the 429 finally became the standard Thunderbird engine. The 390 engine, which had powered Thunderbirds for eight years, was not offered as an option, although it was used in some Fairlanes, Torinos, Mustangs and full-size Fords.

1967 Thunderbird Two-Door Landau

1968 Thunderbird Four-Door Landau

1967 Thunderbird Two-Door Hardtop

1969 Thunderbird Two-Door Landau

THUNDERBIRD AT A GLANCE, 1960-1969										
	1960	1961	1962	1963	1964	1965	1966	1967	1968	1969
Price Range, $	3755-4222	4170-4637	4321-5439	4445-5563	4486-4953	4486-4953	4426-4879	4603-4825	4716-4924	4824-5043
Weight Range, lbs.	3799-3897	3958-4130	4132-4471	4195-4396	4431-4586	4470-4588	4359-4496	4248-4348	4366-4458	4348-4460
Wheelbases, in.	113	113	113	113	113	113	113	115-117	115-117	115-117
8 Cyl. Engines, hp	300-350	300	300-340	300-340	300-330	300-330	315-345	315-345	315-360	360

Imperial

Chrysler and Imperial Division of Chrysler Corp.
Highland Park, Michigan

Virgil M. Exner's heroically finned Imperials of the late 1950s and early '60s were the kind of cars that cause modern stylists to grimace, but they seemed perfectly valid at the time. They sold well, though not in record numbers as they had in 1957. Imperial remained strictly an also-ran among luxury marques. Cadillac held the overwhelming preference of buyers in this market sector, Lincoln was a distant second, and Imperial was an even more distant third.

The Imperials rode Chrysler's largest standard wheelbase of 129 inches. A 149.5-inch wheelbase was used for custom-built Crown Imperial limousines. Unlike other Chrysler products of 1960, Imperials had a separate body and frame. This construction allowed greater insulation to be applied between body and frame, which was necessary, in those days, to achieve the level of smoothness and silence that Imperial buyers demanded. The '60 engine, held over from 1959, was a 413 cubic-inch wedge-head V-8 that developed 350 bhp at 4600 rpm. It required premium fuel, had 10:1 compression, and was the only power plant available for any Imperial.

The 1960 line was identical with that of 1959. Three standard models were offered on the 129-inch wheelbase: the Custom Imperial, the Crown, and the Le Baron. Each series was separated from the next by about $600 in base price. Each included a four-door sedan and hardtop (Southampton) sedan. Two-door Southampton hardtops were available in the Custom and Crown series. The Crown series offered Imperial's only convertible. At their $5,774 base price, few convertibles were sold. Only 618 of them were built for 1960.

Imperial styling for 1960 was a face-lift from 1959. The '60 had a new grille, and a "wrap-over" bright metal roof panel that extended all the way to the

1960 Crown Imperial Ghia Limousine

1961 Imperial Le Baron Four-Door Southampton

1962 Imperial Le Baron Four-Door Southampton

Imperial

windshield. Driver comfort was the big feature for 1960. New features were a high-back driver seat with thick foam rubber padding, adjustable "spot" air-conditioning, a six-way power seat with a single rotary knob control, Auto-Pilot cruise-control, and an automatic headlamp dimmer. The Customs were upholstered in pretty crown-pattern nylon. Crown upholstery was nylon and vinyl, wool, or leather. Wool broadcloth was used in Le Barons.

The long-wheelbase Crown Imperial limousines, built by Italy's Ghia coachworks in 1960-65, followed basic Imperial styling for each model year. Ghia got the assignment because Chrysler could not economically build customs in Detroit. The projected domestic tooling cost was $3.3 million. Ghia could tool Crown Imperials for only $15,000, provided Chrysler could ship the basic "kit" to Ghia's factory in Turin.

Each Ghia limousine began as an unfinished two-door Imperial hardtop on a rigid convertible chassis. This was shipped to Italy with all body panels intact. Ghia cut the car apart, added 20.5 inches to the wheelbase, reworked the structure above the beltline, fitted and trimmed the luxurious interior, and finished off the bodies with 150 pounds of lead filler. Ghia required a month to build each car, and production never totaled more than 16 in any model year of the 1960s. The Crown Imperials were impeccably tailored, all-out luxury cars.

The 1961 Imperial line was altered considerably, though it used the 1960 shell. The fins of '61 were the most blatant ever to appear on an Imperial. They were accompanied by a new gimmick: free-standing headlamps. This was another idea from Exner, who was always influenced by classic cars. The lamps were pocketed in the curve of the front fenders. Free-standing taillights were also used; they dangled from under the towering fins. The strange-looking headlights survived through 1963, but the rear styling was gradually improved during 1962 and 1963. For 1961 the same Custom, Crown, and Le Baron models were offered, but the four-door pillared sedans were eliminated. Again, convertibles were scarce. Only 429 were built.

Exner, who left the corporation during 1961, had envisioned a completely new, truncated Imperial for 1962 to match his downsized Dodges and Plymouths. This car didn't reach production, and that appears fortunate considering the failure of the cheaper '62 makes. The production '62 Imperial's small changes added up to a much improved appearance. The tail fins were shorn down to mere nubs of what they'd been. The new, elongated bullet taillights were free-standing, but they blended better with the rear fenders than the earlier versions had. Predictably, the 1962s sold better than the '61s. Chrysler produced about 600 fewer Customs in 1962, but some 2,200 more Crowns and over 400 more Le Barons. The 413-cid engine for 1962 was rated at 340 hp.

The Imperial received a mild face-lift for 1963. This included a new grille composed of elongated rectangles, a crisp new roofline, and a restyled rear deck. The free-standing taillights were discontinued. The stylist responsible for much of this revision was Elwood Engle, who had replaced Exner in mid-1961. The 1963 roofline, especially, was typical of Engle's squarish designs, and reminiscent of the 1961 Lincoln Continen-

1963 Imperial Crown Four-Door Southampton

1965 Imperial Crown Coupe

1964 Crown Imperial Ghia Limousine

1966 Imperial Crown Convertible

tal he'd styled for Ford. The Imperial lineup for '63 was unchanged, except for the reappearance of the Ghia Crown Imperial, the price of which rose to $18,500. Model year production was about the same as it had been in 1962. Crown convertibles were again the rarest body style: Only 531 were built.

By 1964 model year introduction time, Engle's styling had completely replaced the old Exner silhouette. The Imperial was completely "Continental" in character, its fenderline traced in brightwork like the big Lincolns'. A divided grille appeared, and the free-standing headlamps were discontinued. The Custom model had not sold well, so it was eliminated for '64, along with the Southampton designation for pillarless body styles. This brought the Imperial line down to just five models: the Crown Imperial limousine; the Le Baron hardtop sedan; and the Crown hardtop sedan, coupe, and convertible. The soft top enjoyed its best year of the decade as 922 units were built.

Imperial sales were exceedingly good in 1964. Selling 23,295 units for the model year, Imperial enjoyed its best year since 1957. This performance would not be improved upon until 1969.

Good sales and the big redesign of 1964 dictated a stand-pat season for Imperial in 1965. The only significant change was a new grille with glass-enclosed dual headlights. At the New York Automobile Show, Imperial displayed its exotic Le Baron D'Or show car. The D'Or used gold striping and embellishments, and was painted a special color, Royal Essence Laurel Gold. The usual range was offered. Prices were about $100 to $200 higher than they'd been in 1964. It was another good year: Model year production was 18,409 units, of which 633 were convertibles.

Ghia stopped building limousines in 1965, though 10 more Crown Imperials were constructed in Spain using grilles and rear decks from the '66 models. When Imperial finally went to unit-body construction in 1967, Chrysler worked out a limousine program with Stageway Coaches of Fort Smith, Arkansas. Built from 1967 through 1971 at the rate of about six per year, Stageway cars were called Le Barons rather than Crown Imperials. They were much longer than their predecessors, having an unbelievable 163-inch wheelbase, by far the longest in the American industry. Prices ranged from $12,000 to $15,000, depending on equipment.

Once more in 1966, the Engle line of Crowns and Le Barons was offered with only detail changes. The grille was a cellular affair; each "cell" housed the familiar elongated rectangles. The rear deck was cleaned up by the removal of the fake spare tire cover (a throwback to the Exner years) that had been used in 1965. Back-up lights were inset in the rear bumper. The wheelbase remained at 129 inches. The wedge-head V-8 was bored out to 440 cubic inches and was rated at 350 horsepower. Model year production dropped to 13,752, units, a figure that includes 514 convertibles.

By 1967, Chrysler engineers had had enough experience with unit-body construction to be satisfied

1967 Imperial Crown Coupe

1967 Imperial Le Baron Four-Door Hardtop

1968 Imperial Crown Four-Door Hardtop

1968 Imperial Crown Convertible

with this approach for their most expensive product. Vast technological improvements had also occurred, allowing computerized stress testing of any given unit-body shape before, rather than after, construction. Unit-body construction also cut weight. The 1967 Imperial weighed 100 pounds less than the 1966.

Imperial

The '67s were completely restyled. A new grille with prominent nameplate was accompanied by sharp front fenders that housed parking lights. Headlights were integrated into the grille. There were vertical rear bumpers and horizontal "character lines" along the body sides. Imperial's wheelbase dropped to 127 inches. The four-door pillar-type sedan returned without a model name. It sold for $5,374. The other models continued as in 1966. Convertible production was 577 units. The overall model year total was 17,620 cars.

Volume dropped to 15,367 units for 1968. This caused Chrysler to make a far-reaching decision: For 1969 and beyond, Imperials would share their sheet metal with Chrysler. Among the casualties of this decision was the Crown convertible, which put in its last appearance in 1968. Only 474 copies were built that year. The '68s were altered only slightly from the '67 restyle. The changes included a new grille that extended around the front end to enclose the parking and cornering lights, dual moldings on the lower body sides, and rear side marker lights (required by the federal government). Narrow paint stripes were applied along the beltline on all models. The 440-cid V-8 was still standard. Dual exhausts and twin snorkel air cleaners were offered as an option.

The Chrysler-like cars of 1969 were certainly the cleanest Imperials of the '60s. They had long, low "fuselage styling," a full-width egg-crate grille that concealed the headlamps, and sequential turn signals set into the rear bumper. Ventless side glass was a feature of air-conditioned coupes. Although the 127-inch wheelbase of 1967-68 was retained, new styling lengthened the body of the cars by five inches. The cars also lost about 100 pounds of weight. The engine, as before, was the 350-hp 440 V-8. A hardtop coupe and sedan were offered in both the Crown and the Le Baron series, plus a pillared Crown sedan that was priced identically with the Crown hardtop. Le Baron was no longer the $7,000 semi-custom it had been in past years. Its list price was slashed by about $800. Combined sales of the two Le Barons exceeded those

1969 Imperial Le Baron Four-Door Hardtop

1969 Imperial Le Baron Two-Door Hardtop

1969 Imperial Le Baron Two-Door Hardtop

of the Crown for the first time in history. The cut-price Le Baron was a genuine boost to sales, which reached 22,083 units, the second best figure in Imperial history.

Unfortunately, the Imperial's increasing resemblance to Chrysler during the early 1970s caused sales to drop rapidly. In 1975, Imperial's last year, only about 9,000 were built. The "1976 Imperial" turned out to be a Chrysler New Yorker. Its price was lower and its sales were up. That was fine for the corporation, but sad for tradition.

IMPERIAL AT A GLANCE, 1960-1969										
	1960	1961	1962	1963	1964	1965	1966	1967	1968	1969
Price Range, $	4923-16,500	4923-16,500	4920-6422	5058-18,500	5581-18,500	5772-18,500	5733-18,500	5374-15,000	5654-15,000	5592-15,000
Weight Range, lbs.	4655-5960	4715-5960	4620-4765	4640-6100	4950-6100	5015-6100	4990-6100	4780-6300	4685-6300	4620-6300
Wheelbases, in.	129-149.5	129-149.5	129	129-149.5	129-149.5	129-149.5	129-149.5	127-163	127-163	127-163
8 Cyl. Engines, hp	350	350	340	340	340	340	350	350	350	350

Lincoln

**Lincoln-Mercury Division of Ford Motor Co.
Dearborn, Michigan**

The 1960 Lincoln and Lincoln Premiere were merely extensions of the 1958-59 designs. The new styling consisted of a revised grille and front bumper. The massive bumper guards were moved inward of the canted headlights. The deck was redesigned, with taillights and back-up lights set into a "rear grille" panel, rather than in the rear edges of the fenders as in 1959. The roof and rear window were reshaped, and a full-length body side molding was applied. Standard equipment on both Lincoln and Lincoln Premiere included Twin-Range Turbo-Drive automatic, self-adjusting power brakes, power steering, heater and defroster, whitewall tires, undercoating, clock, windshield washers, radio, remote-control outside mirror, padded instrument panel and sun visors, back-up lights, parking brake warning light, and full wheel covers. Premieres also came standard with a power seat and power windows, and a rear compartment reading light.

The 1960 Lincolns rode a 131-inch wheelbase. They were powered by a 430 cubic-inch V-8 (bore and stroke 4.30 x 3.66 inches), which developed 315 bhp at 4100 rpm. Dual exhausts and aluminized mufflers were used. Each Lincoln series consisted of a four-door sedan, a hardtop sedan (Landau), and a hardtop coupe. Premiere prices started about $500 above those of comparable standard Lincolns. Performance was adequate, but only in a straight line. The Lincoln was a large, heavy car, and it behaved as a softly sprung sedan that weighs 5,000 pounds usually does.

Better things were in the making for 1961. In fact, the generation of sedans, convertibles, and hardtops that began with the '61 was one of the most memorable of the decade. A classically beautiful design was combined with superb engineering to create the most satisfying Lincolns since the prewar K series.

The chiseled styling of the new '61 was the work of seven Ford designers, who in June 1961 received the annual award of the Industrial Designers Institute. They were Eugene Bordinat, Don DeLaRossa, Elwood P. Engle, Gayle L. Halderman, John Najjar, Robert M. Thomas, and George Walker. The IDI, which rarely gives its prize to automobile designers, called the 1961 Lincoln an "outstanding contribution of simplicity and design elegance."

Although the 1961 cars—all called Lincoln Continentals—looked new and unique, they shared tooling forward of the cowl with the new 1961 Thunderbird. This cut the tooling cost for two low-production automobiles in half. However, the 1961 Continental was a big, four-door car on a 123-inch wheelbase; the Thunderbird was a two-door on a wheelbase 10 inches shorter.

Styling of the 1961 and later Lincolns involved a smooth-lined body surface, set off with bright metal fender strips that ran uninterrupted from stem to stern; and a modest grille composed of horizontal and vertical elements. The fenderline emphasis made all four fenders easily visible from behind the wheel, and this helped the driver with road placement. In front view, the roof and greenhouse area sloped inward toward the roof. This provided the greatest angle of "tumble-

1961 Lincoln Continental Sedan

1963 Lincoln Continental Sedan

1962 Lincoln Continental Convertible

1964 Lincoln Continental Lehmann-Peterson Limousine

Lincoln

home" yet designed on a large American luxury car. The unique roof shape was accompanied by the first curved side glass in mass production.

The Continental convertible, which shared the model lineup until 1967, was priced about $600 higher than the hardtop sedan. It was the first four-door convertible since Kaiser-Frazer's abortive 1951 Frazer Manhattan. Unlike the Frazer's, the Lincoln's side glass and window frames slid completely out of sight. So did the convertible top, with the help of 11 relays connecting the mechanical and hydraulic linkage. Most of the convertible hardware was taken from the Ford retractable hardtops of 1957-59.

Aside from their styling, the 1961 and following Lincolns were renowned for their quality of construction. The man chiefly responsible for this was Harold C. MacDonald, chief engineer of Ford's Car and Truck Group. MacDonald created no startling engineering innovations. Rather, he refined and perfected techniques that were already known. The new Lincolns had the most rigid unit body and chassis ever produced, the best sound insulation and shock damping in mass production, extremely close machining tolerances for all mechanical components, an unprecedented number of long-life service components, a completely sealed electrical system, and superior rust and corrosion protection.

Finally, the Continental received the most thorough product testing ever applied by Detroit. Each engine was tested on a dynamometer at 3500 rpm (equal to about 98 mph) for three hours. Then it was torn down for inspection and reassembled. Each automatic transmission was tested for 30 minutes before installation. Each finished car was tested for 12 miles on the road, and had to pass in nearly 200 individual categories. Then, black light was used to visualize a flourescent dye in the cars' lubricants, as a check for oil leaks. As proof of the Continental's invulnerability, Lincoln offered a two-year, 24,000-mile warranty.

Public response to the new Continental was immediate and satisfying. Sales of the 1961s exceeded 25,000 units, and more than 30,000 were produced during both 1962 and 1963. Styling changes for the second and third year were minimal, since Lincoln had declared its intention to make improvements only for function, and not simply for the sake of change. The '62 had a cleaner grille with a narrower central crossbar than the 1961. The 1962 headlamps were not set into the grille, and contours were removed from the front bumper. The '63 had a square-textured grille, a restyled back panel applique, and increased trunk space.

For 1964, Lincoln extended the wheelbase to 126 inches. The cars retained this wheelbase into the

1964 Lincoln Continental Sedan

1965 Lincoln Continental Sedan

1967 Lincoln Continental Coupe

1967 Lincoln Continental Coupe

1968 Lincoln Continental Coupe

1967 Lincoln Continental Sedan

1969 Lincoln Continental Sedan

1968 Lincoln Continental Parade Convertible

1969 Lincoln Continental Presidential Limousine

1970s. The basic styling theme, however, remained unchanged. A convex grille with vertical bars, a wider roof, a broader rear window, and a low-contour convertible top were the only design alterations.

Convertible sales had always been just a small fraction of sedan sales, usually about 10 percent of the whole. Lincoln wanted a more popular body style, and added a two-door hardtop coupe in 1966. The prices of all models were cut. The coupe, at $5,485, was priced lowest. As a result, sales moved sharply upward. The model year total was more than 54,000 units. Although only about 25 percent of Cadillac's figure, this was a Lincoln record.

Also for 1966, the Continental V-8 was bored and stroked to 462 cubic inches (4.38 x 3.83). It developed 340 bhp at 4600 rpm in that form. This engine remained the standard (and only) Lincoln power plant until 1969. Then the cars received the 460 cubic-inch (4.36 x 3.85) V-8 of the Continental Mark III, which offered 365 bhp at 4600 rpm.

The 1965 Lincolns had a new horizontal grille, combination parking and turn signal lights housed in the front fenders, and ribbed taillights.

For 1966 the hood was lengthened, and this increased overall length by about five inches. The rear wheel cutouts were enlarged. A slight hop-up was placed in the rear beltline. A new grille and front bumper were applied. The bumper wrapped back all the way to the front wheel cutouts.

Another grille-and-taillight shuffle, and a spring-loaded hood emblem, distinguished the '67s. The convertible put in its last appearance in 1967, when it sold for $6,449 and saw only 2,276 copies.

During 1967-68, Lehmann-Peterson Company built special-order Continental limousines on a 160-inch wheelbase. Also, Lincoln delivered two custom convertibles to the U.S. Secret Service for official functions. The convertibles, which incorporated a variety of classified features, replaced two other cars that had been in service for a decade. They were equipped with a retractable platform for Secret Service riders. Their rear doors were designed in two sections to allow agents to enter the moving car from the running boards through a 15-inch-wide space. The convertible tops were made of transparent vinyl. A rear-facing seat behind the front seat, advanced electronic communications systems, a PA speaker, a siren, and emergency flasher lights were all part of the specifications.

1969 Lincoln Continental Coupe

Lincoln

In October 1968, Lincoln delivered a Presidential limousine to the White House. This custom had a glass enclosure over the passenger compartment with a hinged center section so the occupants could stand up during a parade. The rear bumper of this 21-foot Continental could be lowered like a tailgate and converted into a platform for Secret Service agents. The limousine had more advanced security, communications, and engineering features than any other automobile ever used by the White House.

Accompanied by the new Continental Mark III coupe, the Lincoln Continental sedan and coupe were the offerings for 1968. The sedan, which had gained roof pillars in 1966, sold for $5,970 base; the coupe was priced at $5,736. The easiest things to change for model identification were the front and rear grilles. They got a new horizontal texture. The front fenders housed three-function lights, for turn signals, parking, and front side markers. The rear lights had four functions: turn signals, brake lights, taillamps, and rear side markers. Their clean design blended well with the fenderlines and allowed Lincoln to avoid clumsy separate side marker lights as a means to meet government mandates.

For 1969, in addition to the emission-certified Mark III V-8 of 365 horsepower, the Continental sedan and coupe received a new, squarish grille, with a center section that extended into the hood area. A Town Car interior was offered. It provided, according to Lincoln's brochure, "unique, super-puff leather-and-vinyl seats and door panels, luxury wood-tone front seat back and door trim inserts, extra plush carpeting and special napped nylon headlining." Government-required safety equipment included a dual hydraulic brake system warning light, four-way emergency flasher, day-night rearview mirror, and energy-absorbing steering column and instrument panel. Continentals retained the 126-inch wheelbase, but their overall length had grown to 224.5 inches.

By the end of the decade, the Lincoln Continental had grown appreciably in size, if not in weight. Sales continued at a respectable level, for the cars had made many friends among luxury car buyers. The Continental had always been a good performer (0 to 60 mph in 11 seconds, top speed 117 mph). Clean design, careful attention to quality control, and conservative but thorough engineering had resulted in a highly desirable luxury automobile.

LINCOLN AT A GLANCE, 1960-1969										
	1960	1961	1962	1963	1964	1965	1966	1967	1968	1969
Price Range, $	5253-5945	6069-6715	6074-6720	6270-6916	6292-6938	6292-6938	5485-6383	5553-6449	5736-5970	5830-6063
Weight Range, lbs.	4917-5064	4927-5215	4966-5370	4936-5340	5055-5393	5075-5475	4985-5480	4940-5505	4883-4978	4910-5005
Wheelbases, in.	131	123	123	123	126	126	126	126	126	126
8 Cyl. Engines, hp	315	300	300	320	320	320	340	340	340	365

CONSUMER GUIDE®

Mercury

Lincoln-Mercury Division of Ford Motor Co.
Dearborn, Michigan

Mercury production during the 1960s involved a plethora of models, sizes, body types, and wheelbases, complicated by several changes in model names from year to year. This is perhaps symbolic of Mercury's mixed fortunes during the period, and the company's struggles to make improvements. Despite the confusion, many familiar Mercury names present at the outset of the decade were still around toward its end. Comet and Monterey spanned the entire 10 years; Montclair and Park Lane were still being built in 1968. Meteor, long a Canadian-made Mercury, was used in two different U.S. applications between 1961 and 1963.

The American Meteor appeared in 1961 as a budget-priced model of the full-size Mercury. A 600 and 800 series were offered. Prices started at $2,535. The Meteor's standard engine was the 223 cubic-inch overhead-valve Ford six, which developed 135 horsepower. Although the Meteor actually outsold the Monterey line in 1961, it was replaced in 1962 by a "Monterey 6." The Meteor name then was moved to a new intermediate, Mercury's version of the Ford Fairlane.

Everything recorded concerning the Fairlane can also be applied to the 1962-63 Meteor. The cars shared the same body (although the Mercury's styling was busier), and came with the small-block 221-cid V-8 as standard. This was supplemented in 1963 by an optional 260-cid small-block for the Meteor Custom and S-33 luxury hardtop. The Meteor didn't sell as well as the Fairlane from the beginning. Accordingly, Mercury dropped the Meteor for 1964 and put all of its compact-car development funds into an extensively face-lifted Comet.

The Comet first appeared with the Ford Falcon in 1960, when it sold over 116,000 copies. Sales increased in 1961, and were strong in 1962. Except for station wagons, Comets had a wheelbase five inches longer than the Falcon's. And one of the reasons the Meteor didn't sell well is that the Comet was comparably sized, yet priced lower. The decision to promote Comet as the only "small Mercury" was a good one. Comet sales jumped by 55,000 units for 1964 and remained high into 1967.

Compared with the Falcon, Mercury's Comet was better trimmed and more elaborately styled, but priced less than $100 higher. Several interesting models were offered. When it became obvious in 1961 that people liked sporty compacts, Mercury introduced the $2,300 S-22 sport coupe. At the same time, all Comets became available with an optional six, which developed 101 hp. For 1962, an S-22 hardtop and convertible were added to the series. The latter was priced at $2,710. As of the squarish face-lift of 1964, the S-22 was renamed Comet Caliente. By then, any

1960 Mercury Colony Park Station Wagon

1961 Mercury Comet Two-Door Sedan

1962 Mercury Comet S-22 Sport Coupe

1962 Mercury Meteor Two-Door Sedan

1963 Mercury Comet Custom Two-Door Hardtop

Mercury

Comet could be equipped with the outstanding 260-cid small-block. For all-out performance, there was a special Cyclone hardtop, which came with the 210-hp, 289-cid V-8 as standard equipment. Mercury inexplicably dropped its Comet wagons for 1964, then reinstated them for 1965.

The Comet got its first major design overhaul in 1966, when it deserted the compact-car field for the intermediate one by use of the sleek new Fairlane body. This move underlined a basic marketing decision: Mercury customers were assumed to be wealthier than Ford buyers and therefore would probably be happier with a car larger than the Falcon. The Comet remained a 116-inch-wheelbase intermediate through 1969. It experienced several lean years along the way.

Gradually, during the late 1960s the name Comet was de-emphasized. In 1967, for example, it appeared only on the very basic "Comet 202" model. The rest of the intermediate line consisted of the Capri, Caliente, Cyclone, and Station Wagon. All these cars were known as the "Cyclone Series."

In 1968, the luxurious Montego line replaced the Caliente, Capri, and Station Wagon. Montegos came in two different configurations: the basic sedan and hardtop coupe priced about $2,550; and the Montego MX sedan, hardtop coupe, convertible and wagon priced from $2,700 to $2,900. Yet another version was the Montego MX Brougham of 1969, an ultra-luxurious series comprising a four-door sedan and hardtop coupe. The MX was outfitted with high-quality cloth upholstery and other luxury details. The name Comet was retained for a $2,500-$2,600 price leader in what was known as the "Montego Series."

The Cyclone and Montego series of Mercury intermediates spawned some of the most roadworthy Mercurys of the decade, including several champion racing cars. After adoption of the Fairlane body in 1966, Mercury offered the Cyclone GT hardtop coupe and convertible. They used Ford's 390-cid V-8, which developed 335 hp, and they offered a variety of useful suspension options. The 1967 Cyclone was even more impressive, since a 427-cid Ford V-8 which provided 410 to 425 horsepower was available as an option. Similar street racers were available in 1968, though the 427 engines were detuned to 390 horsepower that year.

For 1969, Mercury produced an exciting pair of fastback hardtops, the Cyclone and Cyclone CJ. Both had special identification, narrow painted racing stripes, and a unique rear end and taillight design. Options included wide belted tires, turbine-style wheel covers, and competition outside mirrors. The Cyclone CJ had clean sides, no chrome, a blacked-out grille, and a functional hood air scoop for a Ram-Air version of the 428-cid Cobra-Jet engine. Although Ford was NASCAR Grand National Champion in 1968-69, many notable performances were recorded by Cyclones. The best was Cale Yarborough's victory in the 1968 Daytona 500, at a 143.250-mph average.

Mercury's most consistent and steady sales records of the 1960s were made by its standard-size cars. The production level usually attained was 100,000 units, except in those back-to-back record years of 1965 and 1966. Annual production in both '65 and '66 was more than 165,000 of the large Mercurys. Of all the big models, only Monterey spanned the entire decade. The upper-priced Montclair and Park Lane were dropped in 1961, revived for 1964-68, and dropped again in 1969 when they were replaced by the Marquis and Brougham.

The 1960 line of big Mercurys rode a 126-inch

1964 Mercury Comet Cyclone Two-Door Hardtop

1965 Mercury Park Lane Four-Door Sedan

1964 Mercury Montclair Marauder Four-Door Hardtop

1966 Mercury Montclair Two-Door Hardtop

wheelbase. The various models were separated in price by about $500. The standard engine of the Montclair and Park Lane was the Lincoln-based 430-cid V-8, which produced 310 hp. Montereys and Commuter wagons were available with a 312-cid V-8 of 205 hp as standard, and a 383 V-8 of 280 hp as an option. The styling was modest: The cars had a short, concave, full-width grille; a wraparound windshield; and a single bright metal side strip. The Monterey dominated the 1960 selling season.

For 1961, Mercury moved down into the market territory vacated by the Edsel. The Montclair and Park Lane were dropped, as were the high-priced Cruiser hardtops from the Monterey series. Monterey was joined by the aforementioned six-cylinder Meteor. The wheelbase was shortened half a foot to 120 inches. The 430 V-8 was dropped, and a 292-cid, 175-hp engine was the standard V-8. Monterey engine options ran up to a 390-cid power plant, which developed 300 hp. Big-car sales were not spectacular. The Comet, however, had a record model year in 1961, when over 197,000 units were sold. Comet helped Mercury hold sixth place in monthly production during most of 1961, its best performance of the decade.

The Meteor was an intermediate for 1962, so the full-sized line consisted only of Montereys, and Colony Park and Commuter wagons. Mercury moved up-market again with the Monterey Custom. This series included a convertible. Mercury joined the bucket-seat brigade midyear with its Monterey S-55 hardtop coupe and convertible. Styling was busier in 1962, with free-standing taillights and a gaudy grille. The previous lineup of V-8 engines remained, and a 223-cid six that developed 138 hp was offered for the standard Monterey.

Once more in 1963, the Monterey and wagons made up the entire full-size line. Mercury introduced "Breeze-way Styling." This was a rear window with a reverse

slant like that of the old Turnpike Cruiser. The window slid down for enhanced ventilation. Montereys and Monterey Customs were offered again. The wagon line was trimmed to the Colony Park only. A slope-back hardtop coupe and a convertible were added to the S-55 series. The convertible was priced at $3,900.

By '64, tradition had returned. Mercury restored the old lineup of the Monterey, Montclair, and Park Lane, and Commuter and Colony Park wagons. The first three ranges included two-door and four-door hard-tops, four-door sedans, and fastback "Marauder" hardtop sedans. The lineup included a $2,819 Monterey two-door sedan, and a $3,549 Park Lane convertible. The 390 V-8 had become Mercury's standard power plant in 1963. It was accompanied by an optional 427-cid engine, which provided 410 to 425 hp. The 427 was available in all models except the wagons. Marauders with the 425 hp engine were awesome performers.

In record year 1965, the full-size Mercury shared a restyle with Ford. The wagons rode a 119-inch wheelbase; all other standard models rode a 123-inch wheelbase. Breezeway and conventional four-door models were sold in all series, with the usual line of 390 and 427 V-8s. Mercury touted "Torque Box" body construction, frames that were tuned for each body style to minimize noise, vibration and harshness.

In 1966 a new die-cast grille was adopted. Two-door models got a new "sweep-style roof" with a concave backlight—a dramatic move away from the Breezeway design. For 1967, the styling was revised again and the limited-production Marquis was announced. It came as only one model, a two-door hardtop with broad rear roof pillars and vinyl top. It was priced at $3,989. Another innovation was the vinyl-topped Brougham, part of the Park Lane series.

In '68, the Brougham became a separate series. The Marquis and Brougham were limited editions in 1968,

1967 Mercury Cougar

1968 Mercury Cougar XR-7 GTE

1967 Mercury Comet Cyclone GT Two-Door Hardtop

1968 Mercury Montego MX Convertible

Mercury

but in 1969 they replaced the long-running Montclair and Park Lane. Production of the Marquis and Brougham totaled 81,398 units.

A high-performance, low-volume '69 Mercury was the Marauder fastback hardtop, which accounted for 14,666 sales. Its sleek and clean bodywork featured a Marquis grille, concealed headlights, quad taillights, ventless side windows, and full-length racing stripes. About 5,600 Marauders carried the X-100 designation. These models offered styled aluminum six-inch wheels and fender skirts in addition to standard Marauder equipment. The basic Marauder listed for about $3,300; the X-100 was priced almost $800 higher than that. Both Marauders were powered by Mercury's new 429-cid V-8. Two-barrel carburetion gave the engine 320 hp in the basic Marauder; the four-barrel carb of the X-100 raised output to 360 hp.

One of the more interesting and desirable Mercurys of the 1960s was the 111-inch-wheelbase Cougar. It was offered as a hardtop for 1967-68, and as a hardtop and convertible for 1969. Based on the Mustang but riding a wheelbase three inches longer, the Cougar was a deluxe version of Ford's successful "ponycar," priced about $200 above the Ford. The Mustang came with a six-cylinder engine as standard. Cougar's base engine was the 200-hp 289 V-8. Cougar options included a 225-hp 289 V-8 and the big 320-hp 390-cid engine. In 1968, the 390 provided 335 hp; in 1969 a Cougar could be ordered with the CJ 428, also with 335 hp.

The Mercury Cougar was a dashing car, identified in 1967 by its electric-shaver-style grille and hidden headlights. Sequential turn signals had been a Cougar feature from the first models. The vertical grille bars were blacked out in 1968, giving the car a more conventional look. For '69 the body was widened and lengthened, and was given a full-length contour line, ventless curved side glass, a die-cast grille, and

1969 Mercury Montego MX Villager Station Wagon

1969 Mercury Cougar Convertible

full-width taillights. The best of the breed was the glamorous XR-7, which was equipped with a rich leather interior and comprehensive instrumentation set into a simulated walnut dashboard. GT and GTE Cougars powered by the 427 V-8 were offered beginning in 1968 with a variety of handling and performance options. The Cougar never approached the Mustang in sales, but was a boost to Mercury. Production started at 150,000 units for 1967 and remained over 100,000 in 1968 and 1969. It was a more solid, more luxurious, and equally roadable alternative to the Mustang. Among collectors, the appeal of the 1967-68 Cougars has long been acknowledged.

The Cougar had put the finishing touches on a complete reversal of Mercury's image, which by 1967 was one of performance as well as luxury. By the end of the decade, Mercury had successfully reassumed the hot-car image that it had enjoyed in the late '40s and early '50s.

MERCURY AT A GLANCE, 1960-1969										
	1960	**1961**	**1962**	**1963**	**1964**	**1965**	**1966**	**1967**	**1968**	**1969**
Price Range, $	1998-4018	2000-3191	2084-3738	2084-3900	2126-3549	2154-3599	2206-3614	2284-3989	2477-3888	2532-4262
Weight Range, lbs.	2399-4558	2376-3872	2420-4198	2462-4318	2539-4287	2584-4263	2779-4383	2787-4297	2982-4331	3060-4436
Wheelbases, in.	109.5-126	109.5-120	109.5-120	109.5-120	114-120	109.5-123	113-123	111-123	111-123	111-124
6 Cyl. Engines, hp	90	85-135	85-145	85-145	101-116	120	120	120	115	155
8 Cyl. Engines, hp	205-310	175-300	164-300	164-405	164-425	200-425	200-345	200-425	195-390	220-360

Metropolitan

American Motors Corp.
Kenosha, Wisconsin

The whimsical Metropolitan was a car of the 1950s—indeed its origins go back to the late 40s—and the few sold during the 1960s looked out of place. Approved for production in 1952-53, and face-lifted for the first and only time in 1956, the Metropolitan was stubby and broad-shouldered. It had all the worst styling excesses of the last Nash cars, which had disappeared after 1957.

But the Met was appealing to people who needed no more than two seats and space for a couple of sacks of groceries. The British Austin's 91 cubic-inch, 52-horsepower four was adequate to move the almost 1,900-pound car up to 70 miles an hour. More important, it delivered impressive fuel economy of up to 40 miles per gallon. Such attributes were valuable during the small-car awakening that took place in America during the late '50s and early '60s. Metropolitan registrations, which previously had rarely exceeded 10,000 units a year, reached 15,000 in 1957, and 22,000 (the record) in 1959. By then, American Motors was mainly concerned with Ramblers, but the company's management was sufficiently impressed by Metropolitan sales to keep the cars available for a few more years.

The Metropolitan concept dates back to the early postwar years, when George Mason, then president of Nash-Kelvinator, became interested in a design by free-lance stylist Bill Flajole. The tiny prototype evolved into Nash's experimental NXI, and public response was encouraging. Mason thought Nash could have the car built in Europe, import it to America, and sell it at a modest profit. After talking to Triumph and Morris, Mason settled on Austin for the power plant, and Birmingham body builders Fisher & Ludlow for the bodywork. F&L built the Detroit-styled Metropolitans, and shipped them to Austin for installation of the engine and drive train. Then Austin shipped them to the States.

There was no change whatsoever in the Metropolitan during its 1960-62 run. The only model was the

1961 Metropolitan 1500 Hardtop Coupe

1500, which had first appeared in 1956. During the 1960s, the hardtop coupe sold for $1,673; the convertible for $1,697. In 1961-62, a $53 surcharge was tacked onto cars delivered to the West Coast.

What finished off the Metropolitan was the dual onslaught of Volkswagen and the American compacts. By 1961, VW had proved the worth of its prewar-designed Beetle. Detroit, meanwhile, had built a variety of interesting compacts, which held five passengers and lots of luggage, and sold for within $200 of the Metropolitan's price. American Motors reintroduced the compact Rambler American in 1959, and sold it for only $125 more than the Metropolitan.

Metropolitan production was halted in mid-1960. Leftovers accounted for a handful of registered '61 and '62 models. American Motors has only annual registration figures, which may or may not coincide with model year production: 13,103 for 1960; 853 for 1961; and 412 for 1962.

METROPOLITAN AT A GLANCE, 1960-1969										
	1960	1961	1962	1963	1964	1965	1966	1967	1968	1969
Price Range, $	1673-1697	1673-1697	1673-1697							
Weight Range, lbs.	1850-1890	1850-1890	1850-1890							
Wheelbases, in.	85	85	85							
4 Cyl. Engines, hp	52	52	52							

Oldsmobile

**Oldsmobile Division of General Motors Corp.
Lansing, Michigan**

For the longtime "experimental division" of General Motors, the '60s were typical years. Oldsmobile experimented—introducing a variety of new models from compacts to full-size cars, and new engines, and power trains—and its product decisions were rarely mistaken. The division prospered. In annual volume, Oldsmobile never ranked below seventh place, often ranked fourth, and averaged about fifth through the decade. From a calendar year output of

1960 Oldsmobile Super 88 Convertible

1961 Oldsmobile F-85 Cutlass Sports Coupe

1961 Oldsmobile Super 88 Convertible

1962 Oldsmobile Jetfire Sports Coupe

about 402,000 cars in 1960, production rose to 668,000 in 1969.

Oldsmobile joined the producers of compact cars in 1961. The Oldsmobile F-85 and the Cutlass variations that followed set record after record; production in each new model year through 1968 exceeded that of each previous year. This success was due to Oldsmobile's correct matching of customer tastes with new products: compact V-8s in 1961-62; larger compacts with a V-6 option in 1964-65; and the high-performance 4-4-2 series from 1964 on. Every year, Oldsmobile's smallest series seemed to offer a package that was on the money. Its standard-size cars also consistently sold well.

The F-85 was part of the second-wave GM compact program for model year 1961. Buick, Oldsmobile, and Pontiac each developed its own version based on shared bodies and dimensions. Pontiac's Tempest, with its curved drive shaft and rear transaxle, was radical. Oldsmobile took a more conventional route with its F-85 V-8 for the first two years of production. The Olds engine was identical with Buick's: It displaced 215 cubic inches and developed 155 horsepower. It provided good performance (0 to 60 mph in 13 seconds) and reasonable economy (18 mpg). The styling of the F-85 was clean and less busy than that of Buick's Special. It had sculptured body sides, a crisp roofline, and a grille composed of vertical bars, with block letters that spelled Oldsmobile.

Naming the F-85 had been a small problem. Starfire had been the original choice, but that seemed to denote a big sporty car. Rockette was suggested, but was thought to project an unwanted image of the Radio City Music Hall dancers. The numerical designation was inspired by an Olds show car called F-88. The number 85 was chosen because it suggested a family relationship with that show car, yet was far enough away from the 88 designation to avoid confusion. F-85s were offered in standard and deluxe form as sedans, coupes, and wagons. The Deluxe coupe, with bucket seats and luxury trim, was called Cutlass—a name that would supplant the F-85 designation in the 1970s. In the beginning, prices of the F-85s ranged from $2,330 to $2,897.

For 1962, the Cutlass came standard with a 185-hp Power-Pack version of the little 215 V-8. Also available was a new Oldsmobile idea, the turbocharged Jetfire. The turbocharger increased output to 215 hp—one horsepower per cubic inch—but the engine suffered problems including carbon buildup with certain grades of gasoline. To solve these problems, Olds resorted to the unorthodox technique of water injection (actually, a mixture of water and alcohol). The $3,048 Jetfire was remarkably fast (0 to 60 mph in 8.5 seconds, and a top speed of 107 mph), but the injection system proved unreliable. By 1964, Oldsmobile dropped it and gave the F-85 a new engine of 330 cubic-inch displacement, a conventional V-8 that provided 230 to 290 hp. The 225-cid Buick V-6 was added as an option. This six continued unchanged until 1966, when it was replaced with an in-line six of the same horsepower.

The F-85 grew larger through these years, as the public kept insisting on more-impressive "compacts." Its wheelbase went from 112 to 115 inches in 1964, and to 116 (112 for two-doors) in 1968. F-85 bodies grew longer and wider, but the styling actually improved as time went on. The styling of the truncated original was greatly cleaned up in 1963. It was even cleaner in 1964, after a face-lift that gave it a close identity with the full-size Oldsmobiles. In 1966, the straight beltline yielded to a more flowing line, incorporating a hump over the rear wheels. After 1968, F-85 styling began to get cluttered, with a busier grille and deck, and clumsy-looking vinyl tops.

The F-85 that offered the best performance was the exciting 4-4-2. The designation stood for four speeds (or after 1965, 400 cubic inches), four-barrel carburetor, and dual exhausts. In 1964, the 4-4-2 came with a hot 330-cid V-8, heavy-duty suspension, and a four-speed manual gearbox. In 1965, it was hotter still, having been equipped with a 400-cid V-8, an underbored version of the big Olds 425 engine that was used in larger Oldsmobiles. The 4-4-2 option package with four-speed cost only about $250 in 1965. It included heavy-duty wheels, shocks, springs, rear axle, drive shaft, engine mounts, steering and frame; stabilizer bars front and rear; fat tires; special exterior and interior trim; 11-inch clutch; and a 70-amp battery. Its performance was sensational: 0 to 60 in 7.5 seconds; the quarter mile in 17 seconds at 85 mph; a top speed of 125 mph. The 4-4-2 proved, as *Motor Trend* magazine said, "that Detroit can build cars that perform, handle and stop, without sacrificing road comfort. . . ."

Each successive 4-4-2 was eagerly awaited. The 400-cid engine was never pushed much beyond 350 hp, but the cars continued to be good-looking, fast, and great fun to drive. The 1969s had big 4-4-2 numerals on the center grille divider, front fenders, and deck; twin black horizontal grilles; and a unique "two-plateau" hood with special stripes in contrasting paint. They'd become a bit outlandish-looking, perhaps, but they were no less the performance cars than they'd been in the beginning.

By 1966, though, the hot-performing Cutlass and 4-4-2 had been overshadowed by a fascinating new Oldsmobile, the front-wheel-drive Toronado. First offered as a hardtop coupe, the Toronado represented a clean break with the past (and a GM commitment to front-wheel-drive that would become corporate-wide by 1980). It marked a big turnabout for a company that had once panned the front-drive Cord. But GM planned well; the Toronado worked, and worked beautifully.

The goal of the front-wheel-drive exercise was to combine traditional American big-car power with outstanding handling and traction. The front-drive Torona-

1962 Oldsmobile Ninety Eight Convertible

1963 Oldsmobile Starfire Sports Coupe

1963 Oldsmobile Ninety Eight Convertible

1964 Oldsmobile Jetstar 88 Four-Door Sedan

1964 Oldsmobile Cutlass Sports Coupe

1965 Oldsmobile Delta 88 Holiday Sedan

Oldsmobile

do used a 425 cubic-inch, 385-hp V-8 that was also used in the conventional full-size models. Teamed with this power plant was a unique transmission that was divided into two parts. The torque converter was mounted behind the engine, and the gearbox was located under the left bank of cylinders. The two segments were connected by a chain drive and sprocket. The chain drive, virtually unbreakable yet flexible, was developed to cut weight at low cost. It allowed the engineers to create a very compact engine and drive train package. Previous front-drive systems had placed the engine behind the front-mounted transmission. Toronado's split transmission enabled the engine to be placed directly over the front wheels. The result was a front/rear weight distribution of 54/46, which was excellent for a front-wheel-drive car.

Toronado's styling was as sophisticated as its engineering. The roofline fell gently toward the edges of the roof, then dropped in an unbroken curve past the windows, sides, and rocker panels. The curved fuse-lage was set off by boldly flared wheel arches. The front and rear were clean, wrapped as tightly under-neath as were the sides. Don Vorderman, then editor of *Automobile Quarterly* magazine, remarked: "A radically different look has been achieved with a minimum of fuss. There are no loose ends, no unresolved lines. . . . The result is logical, imaginative, and totally unique."

The Toronado was a superb driving machine. It exhibited some understeer, but not much, and ran quietly even at 100 mph. It could do 135 miles an hour when pressed, even with a "standard" rear axle and automatic transmission. It was probably the most outstanding single model of the 1960s. Although the 1968-69 versions were not as cleanly styled as those of '66 and '67, the Toronado was a landmark creation.

While producing the interesting and exciting F-85, Cutlass, 4-4-2, and Toronado, Oldsmobile remained a builder of large, conventional cars. Standard-size models were the division's mainstay. They started off in 1960 with the traditional Oldsmobile lineup: Dynamic 88, the price leader; Super 88, the big-engined performance car of the group; and 98 (also called "Ninety Eight"), the luxury series. The lineup expanded in 1964, when the Jetstar 88 arrived as the lowest-priced model, along with the Jetstar I sports coupe (with concave backlight). To make room for the Jetstar 88, the Dynamic 88 was moved up in the price scale.

In 1965, the Delta replaced the Super, and in 1966, the Jetstar was replaced by the Delmont. The market territory of the Delmonts expanded in '67, eliminating the old Dynamic series. For 1968, the big Olds line went back to its basic three-model range of Delmont, Delta, and 98. Then, in 1969, the Delmont was dropped and Delta 88s were offered in three stages of luxury: standard, Custom, and Royale.

The broad range of body styles of most large Oldsmobiles of the '60s included hardtop coupes and sedans, convertibles, the Vista Cruiser (with transparent rooflights), and Fiesta station wagons. Their design was clean in 1960, cleaner in 1961, and spectacularly handsome ("Straightaway Styling") in 1962. Though face-lifts brought rounder, fatter bodies in 1965, each new Oldsmobile retained a visual

1966 Oldsmobile Toronado

1966 Oldsmobile 4-4-2 Sports Coupe

1967 Oldsmobile Ninety Eight Luxury Sedan

1967 Oldsmobile Cutlass Station Wagon

similarity to its predecessor. In 1968-69 the wide, square 1962-64 grille reappeared. In between was an era of broad, pointed noses, single-bar grilles, and prominent quad headlights. Visual identity was maintained through the use of just two wheelbases, 123 and 126 inches, from 1960 to 1968. An inch was added to each wheelbase in 1969. Some of the nicest Oldsmobiles of the decade were sold in '69, when the division called them "The Youngmobiles."

Oldsmobile entered the 1960s with two V-8s: a 371-cid, 240-hp power plant for the Dynamic 88; and a 394-cid, 315-hp engine for the Super 88 and 98. The 394 was the only big-car engine for 1962-63. In '64 the low-priced Jetstar models shared the F-85's new 330 engine. In '64, the 394 came with 280 horsepower standard; 330 hp optional; and 345 hp in the Jetstar I, Starfire, and 98.

In 1965, the 394 was stroked out to 425 cubic inches, to provide 310 hp standard, 360 hp as an option, and 370 hp in the Jetstar I and Starfire. Power rose to 385 hp for the 1966-67 Toronado. It decreased slightly across the board in 1968-69 with the advent of emission controls. The Delmont, which replaced the Dynamic 88 in 1967, started out with the F-85's 330-cid V-8. Both models were bored out to 350 cid (250 hp) for 1968-69.

The Starfire of 1961-66 and the Jetstar I of 1964-65 were Oldsmobile's flings in the market of bucket-seated large cars. The Starfire began as a limited edition, but production was boosted to 41,988 cars for the 1962 model year. Equipped with the highest-power engines, Starfire hardtops and coupes sold for $4,000 to $5,000. They featured individual styling, with broad sweeps of brushed aluminum in the early models; bucket seats with center console; and luxurious interiors. The Jetstar I was the same idea, sold at a more popular price of $3,600. But it didn't catch on; production totaled only 16,084 units for 1964 and 6,552 units for 1965. Although neither the Starfire nor the Jetfire met the true definition of sports cars (as Oldsmobile often referred to them), they were good-handling cars for their size, and they offered distinctive transportation.

1968 Oldsmobile Toronado

1968 Oldsmobile Delmont 88 Holiday Sedan

1969 Oldsmobile Toronado

1969 Oldsmobile Ninety Eight Holiday Coupe

OLDSMOBILE AT A GLANCE, 1960-1969										
	1960	1961	1962	1963	1964	1965	1966	1967	1968	1969
Price Range, $	2835-4362	2330-4647	2403-4744	2403-4742	2343-4753	2344-4778	2348-4812	2410-4869	2512-4750	2561-4835
Weight Range, lbs.	4026-4506	2541-4445	2599-4428	2599-4367	2894-4337	2940-4286	2951-4443	3014-4362	3062-4278	3082-4288
Wheelbases, in.	123-126	112-126	112-126	112-126	115-126	115-126	115-126	115-126	112-126	112-127
6 Cyl. Engines, hp					155	155	155	155	155	155
8 Cyl. Engines, hp	240-315	155-325	155-345	155-345	230-345	250-370	250-385	250-385	250-400	250-400

Plymouth

Chrysler-Plymouth Division of Chrysler Corp.
Highland Park, Michigan

As were the 1950s, the '60s were a decade of ups and downs for Chrysler Corporation's best-selling marque. Plymouth had barely recovered third place in production in the late 1950s when it was knocked out by Rambler. A line of slow-selling intermediates and no standard-sized alternative caused Plymouth to drop to as low as eighth place in the early '60s. The marque recovered in 1964, but could not dislodge Pontiac from third place, and was passed by Buick and Oldsmobile in 1969. These problems were of Plymouth's own doing. Time and again, the division's management failed to correctly gauge the market. Plymouth produced the right cars, but at the wrong time.

The difficulties began at the top of the line. Plymouth marketed a garish tail-finned line of Savoy, Belvedere, Fury and Suburban models for 1960. Although Plymouth's new 225-cid slant-six engine was a good one, Rambler campaigned with conservative styling and more economical sixes, and outproduced Plymouth by 2,000 units for the calendar year. In 1961, Chrysler designer Virgil Exner drastically restyled his cars. The Plymouth was clumsy, marked by a strange, pinched grille and ponderous pod-like taillights. The result was a seventh-place finish for Plymouth, as Pontiac, Oldsmobile, and Mercury swept by on the strength of their big-car sales and successful new compacts.

In 1962 came Plymouth's worst mistake of the decade. Anticipating a strong demand for compact "standard" cars, the company shaved up to eight inches from the Plymouth's wheelbase and 550 pounds from its weight. The line of Savoys, Belvederes, Furys and Suburbans all appeared on a 116-inch wheelbase, and had Valiant-like styling. Plymouth's engines—a 225-cid six that developed 145 horsepower, a 318-cid V-8 of 230 to 260 hp, a Golden Commando 361-cid V-8 of 305 hp, and a 413-cid V-8 of 410 hp—provided fine performance in these light cars. But that didn't make any difference. A public still hungry for large cars from the Big Three shunned Plymouth and looked to Ford or Chevrolet. Hasty face-lifts took place. A more conventional grille with razor-edged fenderlines and squared-off styling was used in 1963; a Chevy-like grille and increased side decoration appeared in 1964. These changes didn't help much, either. Plymouth's rebound to fourth place in 1964 was largely due to the success of its Valiant compact rather than to any increased demand for the revamped large cars.

Plymouth's renaissance really began in 1965, when the division returned to the big-car fold with a 119-inch wheelbase (121 inches for station wagons). The big-car line was led by Furys in four series: Fury I, II, III, and Sport Fury. They were the largest Plymouths ever offered, bigger in wheelbase, overall length, and width than the 1964 models. Interior dimensions were greatly increased. Like all Plymouths since 1960, these cars had unitized body-chassis construction. But the '65s also had a bolt-on subframe to carry the engine and front suspension.

Plymouth had retained its 116-inch-wheelbase intermediates, which by '65 were more in tune with buyer demand. These intermediates, designated Belvederes, were restyled to resemble the Furys. They had a squared-off roofline, clean sides, and a stamped grille. There were Belvedere I and II sixes and V-8s, a Belvedere I Super Stock hardtop, and a top-line

1960 Plymouth Fury Two-Door Hardtop

1960 Valiant V200 Four-Door Sedan

1961 Plymouth Fury Convertible

1962 Plymouth Valiant Signet 200 Two-Door Hardtop

Satellite hardtop and convertible. Standard on the Super Stock (and optional on other Belvederes and Furys) was a 426-cid wedge-head engine that developed 365 hp and 470 foot-pounds of torque. The Super Stock had a special 115-inch wheelbase, and weighed just 3,170 pounds. Its mighty engine provided terrific performance. The car's top speed was about 120 mph, and it could run 0 to 60 mph in eight seconds. But the Super Stock was not cheap at its $4,671 base price. It was intended primarily for racing, and could be ordered with a hemi-head 426 as well as the wedge-head.

For 1966 the incredible 425-hp Hemi was made available as an option on the Belvedere II and Satellite. The result was the electrifying "Street Hemi." The car came with heavy-duty suspension and oversize brakes. It was first offered with a four-speed gearbox; later with the option of Torque-Flite automatic. Since the '66 Belvedere was shorter and lighter than the '65, the Street Hemi could be a docile tourer at low speeds and a demon when stirred up. Equipped with the proper tires and axle ratio, and correctly tuned, it could do 120 mph in 12 or 13 seconds. Street Hemis right off the floor were ready for drag-race competition in A/Stock or AA/Stock classes. They and Dodge's Coronet were allowed to run on NASCAR's shorter circuits in 1966, with predictable results. David Pearson won the '66 NASCAR championship for Dodge, and Richard Petty won in '67 for Plymouth. Petty also won the 1964 Daytona 500 in a Plymouth Hemi. These were the two major breakups of Ford's otherwise tight stranglehold on NASCAR between 1965 and 1970.

The Satellites and Belvedere IIs were elegant-looking cars. When equipped with smaller engines of 273, 318, and 361 cubic-inch displacement, they were among the best all-around Plymouths. Their crisp, clean styling was retained for 1967. In that year, the Hemi option was offered for the Belvedere GTX, along with a 440-cid wedge-head V-8 of 375 hp. GTXs looked the part: They had a silver-and-black grille and rear deck appliqués, simulated hood air intakes, sport striping, and dual exhausts.

In 1968 Plymouth restyled its intermediate, using lines that were more rounded than before, but just as pretty. The hottest model was ingenuously named Road Runner. It was available as a hardtop or coupe. The latter was a European-looking machine with narrow pillars and flip-out rear quarter windows. Road Runner nameplates and cartoon birds on the sides and rear, plus simulated hood scoops and racy wheels, ornamented the car. Squeezed under the hood was either a 383-cid engine, using a 440 intake manifold and heads, or a 426 hemi. The same beefy suspension and four-speed transmission options of the GTX were available for the Road Runner. On street or track, the car was dynamite. Extraordinary as it seems, this finely tuned package of power and performance was available for only $2,800 to $3,100.

In addition to the Road Runner, the GTX continued in hardtop and convertible form for 1968, along with the more mundane Belvedere, Satellite and Sport Satellite

1963 Plymouth Valiant V100 Two-Door Sedan

1964 Plymouth Sport Fury Convertible

1965 Plymouth Barracuda

1965 Plymouth Belvedere I Station Wagon

1966 Plymouth Belvedere II Convertible

sedans, coupes and wagons. Similar models prevailed in 1969, but a $3,318 Road Runner convertible was added to the lineup.

Full-size Plymouths continued to use the 119-inch wheelbase through the rest of the decade (wagons

Plymouth

1967 Plymouth Valiant Signet Four-Door Sedan

1967 Plymouth Barracuda Formula "S"

1967 Plymouth Belvedere I Two-Door Sedan

1968 Plymouth VIP Four-Door Hardtop

1968 Plymouth Barracuda Convertible

rode slightly longer wheelbases). Fury I, II, and III models were offered with sixes and V-8s. Sport Fury hardtops, convertibles, and fastbacks came with V-8s in 1967-68. The top-of-the-line model in 1966 was the VIP, which had a "formal" roofline and conservative trim, and came as a hardtop coupe or sedan. Basic Fury engines were the 225-cid slant six of 145 hp, and the 318-cid V-8 of 230 hp. Options in 1965 included a 361 that developed 265 hp, a 383 of 325 hp, and a 426 of 365 hp. In 1966 a 440 wedge-head replaced the 426. From 1967 on, the optional big-blocks were the 383 of 270 to 330 hp, and the 440 of 375 hp (350 hp in '67 wagons).

Plymouth's salvation in its poorer years of the '60s was the compact Valiant, which had been a make in its own right for 1960, and was a Plymouth model after that. The 1960-62 Valiants were ruggedly built, unit-body cars. Their Virgil Exner styling included pronounced fenderlines, short decks, and square grilles. They rode a 106-inch wheelbase. Elwood Engle's clean, square styling was featured on a 106-inch wheelbase for 1963-66. Styling became more elegant as the years went by. Then in 1967, the line was completely redesigned again. It adopted a 108-inch wheelbase and foursquare lines that were reminiscent of some middle-size European sedans. Valiant remained in this form, the top seller among Detroit compacts, until it was replaced by the Volare in the mid-1970s.

One of Valiant's strong points was its robust slant-six engine. The unit was developed out of the need for a low hoodline, but engineers also claimed certain manufacturing and operational efficiencies for the configuration. In stock form, the 170-cid engine produced 101 hp, though a four-barrel carburetor option for 1960-61 called Hyper-Pack raised output to 148 bhp. A larger, 225-cid version was standard on larger Plymouths in 1960-61. From 1962 on, the 225 was the optional Valiant engine as well. It developed 145 hp. A long-lived design of great durability, the 225 is still being used today in Plymouth products.

Valiants were straightforward and had conventional suspensions. They were offered initially in two series—the V100 and V200. Sedans and wagons only were offered in 1960. A hardtop was available from 1961 on. A hardtop called Signet was the Valiant answer to bucket-seat challenges from Falcon and Corvair. When Engle styling appeared in 1963, the Signet became available as a convertible as well as a hardtop.

The success of the Corvair Monza and Ford Falcon Futura prompted Plymouth to take aim at the sporty-compact market, and in mid-1964, Plymouth introduced the Barracuda for the '65 model year. This fastback version of the Engle Valiant was a hasty tooling revision, carried out on the Valiant's upper body structure. The result was a fastback, made of a huge piece of curved glass behind a rakish roofline. Barracudas came standard with the 225 slant six; a V-8 version was optional, and desirable. This V-8 was a brand-new design, a rival for Ford's excellent 260/289. It displaced 273 cubic inches and was oversquare (bore and stroke

76

3.63 x 3.31 inches). In base form, its horsepower was 180. A 235-hp version was also available. The 235 had a high-lift, high-overlap camshaft; dome-shaped pistons; solid lifters; dual-contact breaker points; an unsilenced air cleaner; and a sweet-sounding, low-back-pressure exhaust system. With Rallye Suspension (heavy-duty torsion bars and anti-sway bars up front, and stiff rear leaf springs), Firm-Ride shocks and a four-speed gearbox, the 235-hp Barracuda cost only $3,400. It would do 0 to 60 in eight seconds flat and the quarter mile in 16 seconds.

The Barracuda's fold-down rear seat could be used to increase luggage capacity. The car offered a combination of sporty looks, high performance, good handling, utility, and room for four. It was the most popular Plymouth for model year 1965: Almost 65,000 units were built.

For 1966, the Barracuda was face-lifted with an egg-crate grille. For 1967, it was completely redesigned. Its wheelbase was lengthened by two inches, and its overall length was increased by five inches. A sleek hardtop coupe and convertible joined the fastback. Plymouth's 383-cid V-8 with four-barrel carb, detuned to 280 hp, became available.

The 383 did boost the Barracuda's performance, and added up to 300 pounds to its weight, mostly over the front wheels. The 273 V-8 was a better choice. Either V-8 could be ordered with a Formula S package, which included heavy-duty suspension, centrally mounted tachometer, Goodyear Wide-Oval tires, and special identification. Base prices for '67 Barracudas were $2,449 for the hardtop, $2,639 for the fastback, and $2,779 for the convertible. They were bargains.

Fortunately, the Barracudas were not drastically changed in the ensuing two years. A vertical-bar grille appeared in 1968, and a checkered grille and redesigned taillights came along in '69. The 273 V-8 was relegated to Valiants and Satellites; the 230-hp 318 became the standard Barracuda V-8. In both years beefy, big-block models, the 'Cuda 340 and 383, were available. The former had 275 hp; the latter offered 300 hp in 1968 and 330 hp in 1969.

1969 Plymouth Fury III Four-Door Hardtop

1969 Plymouth 'Cuda 340

1969 Plymouth GTX Two-Door Hardtop

The Barracuda was completely redesigned, shortened and widened in 1970. Somehow the lines became less distinctive than those of the 1967-69 generation. For buyers in the '60s, as for collectors of today, the 1967-69 seems to be the outstanding vintage. They were clean, lithe-looking cars, well-finished and solidly built. Equipped with the right options, they were outstanding road cars. If not the epitome of grand touring, Formula S Barracudas came close enough to it to satisfy most enthusiasts. And unlike the Mustang, the Barracuda didn't take sales away from its maker's other models.

PLYMOUTH AT A GLANCE, 1960-1969										
	1960	1961	1962	1963	1964	1965	1966	1967	1968	1969
Price Range, $	2053-2990	1955-3136	1930-3082	1910-3082	1921-3095	2004-4671	2025-3251	2117-3279	2301-3543	2307-3718
Weight Range, lbs.	2635-4020	2595-3995	2480-3440	2515-3590	2540-3630	2560-4200	2600-4165	2645-4135	2655-4100	2656-4173
Wheelbases, in.	106.5-122	106.5-122	106.5-116	106-116	106-116	106-121	106-121	108-122	108-122	108-122
6 Cyl. Engines, hp	101-148	101-148	101-145	101-145	101-145	101-145	101-145	115-145	115-145	115-145
8 Cyl. Engines, hp	230-305	230-330	230-410	230-420	230-425	180-425	180-425	180-425	190-425	190-425

Pontiac

Pontiac Division of General Motors Corp.
Pontiac, Michigan

Pontiac was named Car of the Year three times by *Motor Trend* magazine in the 1960s. Some say that that award is often breathlessly bestowed on ordinary cars or worse, but Pontiac truly deserved the title. Piloted by engineering-oriented general managers like Semon E. "Bunkie" Knudsen and Pete Estes, Pontiac Division in the '60s was the home of high performance. The 1950s image of staid family cars had vanished. Again and again throughout the '60s, Pontiac introduced exciting automobiles: the unique 1961 Tempest, the Wide-Track 1962 Grand Prix, the swift and powerful 1964 GTO, the 1966 Tempest overhead-cam six, and the sporty 1967 Firebird. All were interesting cars; some were great cars. Today, most of them are collectors' items.

With all due respect to the full-size Pontiacs, most of the revolutionary news was made by the compact Tempest and the intermediate into which it evolved. The original '61 Tempest won the first Car of the Year award for three reasons: It had GM's first postwar four-cylinder engine, a radical and unprecedented flexible drive shaft, and a transaxle (a combination of rear axle and rear independent-link-type suspension). *Motor Trend* said the new Tempest "sets many new trends and unquestionably is a prototype of the American car for the Sixties . . . ." That summary was wrong on both counts: Nobody copied the drive shaft or transaxle (unless you count the Porsche 928 of 15 years later); and not until the late 1970s was there a strong Detroit shift to four-cylinder engines. The public bought many 1961-63 Tempests, but even more of

their more conventional successors. Tempest's 195 cubic-inch four was abandoned for an in-line six in 1964, which in concept was hardly new. Pontiac built it by chopping one bank of cylinders of its standard 389-cid V-8—clever, but not innovative.

The Tempest drive shaft could be likened to a speedometer cable, in that it transmitted rotary action around a bend, or at least a slight curve. It was a long torsion bar, bent in an arc under the floor—thin, but lightly stressed. It was mounted on bearings and was permanently lubricated inside a steel case. The bent shaft eliminated the floor hump in the front, but not in the rear. It also eliminated universal joints and allowed for softer mounting of the engine, which isolated vibration from the interior.

The Tempest transaxle was a first for Detroit (but not for the world). Aside from allowing for an ostensibly superior independent rear suspension, it made the Tempest less nose-heavy than the Olds F-85 or Buick Special. At the same time, the suspension caused oversteer, which could be especially alarming on wet roads. Yet the car handled well generally, and tracked safely in mud and snow. Use of the standard Buick-Olds-Pontiac compact body gave 1961-63 Tempests a 112-inch wheelbase.

The four had a variety of tune stages. Horsepower depended on whether an engine took regular or premium gas, and whether it was used with manual or automatic transmission. Over the three year period, horsepower ranged from 110 to 166 hp. The 1961-62 models also offered the GM 215-cid V-8, which

1960 Pontiac Bonneville Vista Four-Door Hardtop

1961 Pontiac Tempest LeMans Sport Coupe

1960 Pontiac Catalina Vista Four-Door Hardtop

1962 Pontiac Catalina Vista Four-Door Hardtop

produced 185 hp. The 1963 models used a 264-hp 326. Tempest 326s were quick cars, capable of 0 to 60 times of 9.5 seconds and a top speed of 115 mph.

At first, only one model range of two-door and four-door sedans, a coupe, a convertible, and a Safari wagon was offered.

In 1963, a separate LeMans series included a sport coupe and convertible with bucket seats and deluxe interior trim. Different grilles identified the models of each year. The grille had a separate and semi-oval style for 1961, was full width in three sections for 1962, and was separate but squared off in 1963. For '65, GM lengthened its compact wheelbase to 115 inches, and Pontiac redesigned its model, using taut, geometrical lines. Good styling and numerous high-performance models won Pontiac its second Car of the Year award in 1965.

A mid-1964 introduction destined for greatness was the Tempest GTO, the first of what soon became known as the "muscle cars." The nickname was well taken. Equipped with the proper options, GTOs could provide unprecedented performance for a six-passenger automobile. Of course, GTOs could be ordered in relatively mild-mannered form, with automatic transmission, a 335-hp engine, and so on. The trick was to use the option book wisely. You'd start with a Tempest LeMans at $2,500. The GTO package—floor shift, 389-cid engine, quick steering, stiff shocks, dual exhaust, and premium tires—cost about $300. The four-speed gearbox was $188. Another $75 bought a package comprising metallic brake linings, a heavy-duty radiator, and a limited-slip differential. And an additional $115 would get you the 360-hp engine. At that point, all you needed was a lead foot and lots of gasoline. (And why not, at 30 cents a gallon?)

Sports-car folk took umbrage at Pontiac's use of GTO (*gran turismo omologato*), an international term for production-class racing cars. *Car and Driver* magazine brazenly took issue with those critics by comparing Pontiac's GTO with Ferrari's. A good Pontiac, they said, would trim the Ferrari in a drag race and lose on a road course. But "with the addition of NASCAR road racing suspension, the Pontiac will take the measure of any Ferrari other than prototype racing cars....The Ferrari costs $20,000. With every conceivable option on a GTO, it would be difficult to spend more than $3,800. That's a bargain."

The 115-inch-wheelbase Tempests changed little in ensuing years. Vertical headlights and crisp styling on a three-inch-longer body appeared for 1966. A curving beltline and a divided vertical-bar grille were featured for 1967. In 1968, the cars adopted GM's dual wheelbases of 116 inches for four-doors and 112 inches for two-doors. The '68s followed the styling of the big Pontiacs by adopting a large combination bumper and grille. The '68 GTO's standard engine was a 400-cid V-8 that developed 350 hp. The car could also be ordered with 360 horsepower, by way of a Ram-Air hood scoop. The '68 GTOs were equipped with an energy-absorbing rubber bumper, neatly blended into the body lines. For this feature mainly, Pontiac won another Car of the Year award in 1968. The 1969 models were face-lifted, and became cleaner in style than the '68s. The hottest '69 GTO was "The Judge," which had a 366-hp Ram-Air V-8 and three-speed manual Hurst-shift gearbox.

Pontiac had used an Oldsmobile 140-hp six for 1964-65. Then the division introduced a surprise engine for the '66 Tempest. It was an overhead-cam six, the first performance six since the Hudson Hornet. Although it was not in a league with hairier GTOs, the six was satisfying. It could run 0 to 60 in 10 seconds flat and hit a top speed of 115 mph.

The ohc six displaced 230 cubic inches, developed

1963 Pontiac Bonneville Convertible

1965 Pontiac Bonneville Convertible

1964 Pontiac GTO

1965 Pontiac 2+2 Convertible

Pontiac

1966 Pontiac LeMans Two-Door Sport Coupe

1967 Pontiac Bonneville Four-Door Hardtop

1967 Pontiac Firebird Sport Coupe

1968 Pontiac LeMans Four-Door Hardtop

1968 Pontiac Grand Prix

either 165 hp standard or 207 in Sprint form with Rochester Quadra-Jet carburetor, hot valve timing, and double valve springs. The crankshaft had seven main bearings; the camshaft was driven by a fiberglass-reinforced notched belt rather than the conventional chain or gear drive. The optional four-speed transmission, clean styling, and an interior that featured bucket seats and console gave the Tempests powered by the ohc six the look and feel of an unabashed driver's car. Its life span was short. By 1968, the Tempest had grown bulky, and by 1970, the engine had been emasculated by emission controls and detuning. But it was good while it lasted.

Since Pontiac had such a good reputation for performance and handling, division managers knew that the Firebird "ponycar," based on the Chevrolet Camaro, had to be something special. Firebird used the Camaro's 108-inch wheelbase, but had its own divided grille, and a 325-hp 400-cid V-8 as standard. It was listed at only $2,666 for the coupe and $2,903 for the convertible. Among the optional engines was the overhead-cam six, which made the Firebird a sprightly yet economical performer. Changes were slight in subsequent model years. Side marker lights were added in 1968. The lower body styling and grille were revised and a host of government-ordered safety features were added in '69. Convertible Firebirds continued to be offered until the model was redesigned with the coupe-only bodywork for 1970. Firebirds rarely sold for more than $3,300. They were performance cars designed to be enjoyed by good drivers.

The full-size Pontiacs of the 1960s cannot be ignored, because they were among the better-styled, better-handling large cars of the decade. The public knew this, and responded enthusiastically. Model year production for 1960 had been about 396,000 large cars. In 1969, Pontiac was building close to half a million standard-size sedans, hardtops, convertibles, and wagons. In calendar year output, Pontiac ran third to Chevrolet and Ford from 1962 through 1969. Full-size cars had a lot to do with this success.

Pontiac originally had a four-model approach to the large-car market. The 1960-61 range, from bottom to top, consisted of Catalina, Ventura, Star Chief, and Bonneville. The first two models used a 122-inch wheelbase; the last two, a 124. As the new body was being readied for 1961, the wheelbases were changed to 119 and 123 inches.

In 1962, the Ventura was dropped, and its place was taken by the bucket-seated, limited-edition Grand Prix. This was an elegantly tailored hardtop coupe that had crisp styling and svelte good looks. It rapidly gained in popularity. By 1969, the Grand Prix was outselling all large Pontiac models except Catalina—with a single body style. A convertible was offered in 1967 only. These convertibles are now collectors' items, since only 5,856 were built.

The styling of standard-size Pontiacs kept improving, at least through 1966. The distinctive Pontiac split grille, first introduced in '59 and dropped for '60, was reintroduced in 1961. Clean designs with narrow, split grilles were the style for 1963 and 1964. The 1965s were equally well executed, but had a prominent, bulging grille. This was improved in 1966. Bulkier designs with heavy, curved rear fenderlines arrived in 1967. A huge combination bumper and grille was used in '68. The front end was greatly improved for 1969. The Star Chief Executive had been introduced in 1965. From 1966 on, it was known simply as the Executive.

Catalina and Grand Prix always rode the smaller Pontiac wheelbase. The Grand Prix's wheelbase was shortened to 118 inches for 1969. Bonnevilles and Star Chiefs/Executives rode the longer wheelbase. Each model, separated from the others by a few hundred dollars, offered a comprehensive range of body styles.

Pontiac's big-car engines, though offered in numerous horsepower ratings, comprised just two sizes in the 1960s. The smaller was a 389-cid V-8 (400 cubic inches after 1967). It was standard on all models. Its horsepower ranged from 215 on up to 350 on large Pontiacs. The 350 version was standard on the 1967-69 Grand Prix. The larger engine, optional on most large Pontiacs, displaced 421 cubic inches in 1963-66 and 428 thereafter. It began with 353 hp in 1963, and reached 376 hp by 1967. It was available for the Catalina and Executive as well as for the Bonneville, and provided exhilarating performance in the lighter cars. Also, a 421-cid, 427-bhp engine for drag racing was offered in 1963-64 in a special Catalina that had aluminum body parts, plastic side windows, and drilled-out frames.

Pontiac never reached one horsepower per cubic inch as did GM's other divisions, but its big-block V-8 was more than adequate to make suitably equipped models very fast. The Wide-Track chassis and taut suspensions combined to make those cars roadable as well.

Luxury, performance, comfort and handling in a full-size car plus consistent innovation in compacts and intermediates—no manufacturer did it better than Pontiac in the '60s.

1968 Pontiac Executive Safari Wagon

1969 Pontiac Bonneville Convertible

1969 Pontiac Grand Prix

PONTIAC AT A GLANCE, 1960-1969										
	1960	1961	1962	1963	1964	1965	1966	1967	1968	1969
Price Range, $	2631-3530	2113-3530	2186-3624	2188-3623	2259-3633	2260-3632	2278-3747	2341-3819	2461-3987	2510-4104
Weight Range, lbs.	3835-4365	2785-4185	2785-4220	2810-4245	2930-4275	2930-4310	3040-4390	3110-4415	3242-4485	3180-4600
Wheelbases, in.	122-124	112-123	112-123	112-123	115-123	115-124	115-124	108-124	108-124	108-125
4 Cyl. Engines, hp		110-155	110-166	115-166						
6 Cyl. Engines, hp					140	140	165-207	165-215	175-215	175-230
8 Cyl. Engines, hp	215-318	155-318	185-348	215-427	250-427	250-376	250-376	250-376	265-390	265-390

Rambler
American Motors Corp.
Kenosha, Wisconsin

Rambler's story is ironic. At one point in the 1960s, the Rambler, the pioneer compact car, had the highest sales volume ever recorded for an independent auto maker. The car was perfect for its market. But, as a result, AMC became *too* successful. The Rambler's success thus triggered an avalanche of compacts from the Big Three.

At the beginning of the decade, everything looked rosy. Led by its hard-driving president, George Romney, Rambler could do no wrong. In 1960 it edged past Plymouth into third place in production, with nearly half a million cars. It held onto third place in 1961. But a downward slide began in 1962, when Rambler was passed by Oldsmobile and Pontiac. By 1967, AMC as a whole was in 10th place.

Perhaps Romney saw the handwriting on the wall: He left the company in 1962. The new president was Roy Abernethy, who began a program of product diversification. AMC tried to meet the competition on every front. This didn't work. Abernethy was replaced by Roy D. Chapin, Jr., in 1966. Chapin became AMC board chairman in 1967, and William V. Luneberg became president. The Chapin-Luneberg administration ordered more diversification. It added new makes like the Javelin, and dropped the Rambler name after 1969.

The 108-inch-wheelbase, unit-body Rambler on which AMC built its early success had first appeared in 1956, as a model of Hudson and Nash. It became an individual make in 1957 and was extensively face-lifted through the years. By 1960 it had acquired uncluttered lines, little tail fins, and a full-width grille. Face-lifts occurred in 1961 and 1962, and the cars became known as Rambler Classics. A lower '61 hoodline was accompanied by an egg-crate grille. In 1962 the crate held larger eggs and the cars got a higher side sweep-spear. An interesting '62 option was the E-stick, a combination automatic and clutch transmission that cost $60. But it was too complex a notion to sell really well. (AMC's E-stick was similar to the twin-stick system of today's Dodge Colt FF and Plymouth Champ made by Mitsubishi.)

Richard A. Teague joined the American Motors design staff in 1961, so the first cars he was able to influence were the '63 Classics. Teague used a longer (112-inch) wheelbase and a lower silhouette than before, a concave grille, sculptured body panels, and curved side glass to create a smooth new shape. Although still chunky, the new Rambler was at least cleanly styled. The Classic retained this basic body shape throughout its life span.

Through the years, Teague made further refinements to the Classic. The 1964s had a new flat grille and stainless-steel-trimmed rocker panels. Two hardtop coupes were added to the line, which until 1964 had consisted of two-door and four-door sedans and

1960 Rambler American Super Four-Door Sedan

1961 Rambler American Custom Convertible

1960 Rambler American Super Two-Door Station Wagon

1961 Rambler Classic Cross-Country Four-Door Wagon

four-door Cross Country station wagons. The 1965s got a new grille, a squared-off hood, and wraparound taillights. The 1966 line featured a new roof with convertible-like accents, a revised roof and tailgate for the station wagon, and more sharply creased lines from front to rear.

In 1967 the Rambler Classic was renamed Rebel. From 1968 on, the Rebel was a separate make (see the American Motors chapter); the Rambler marque applied to only the smaller American models. The '67 Rebel got a two-inch longer wheelbase. Its face-lift comprised a floating rectangular grille flanked by horizontal dual headlamps, and squarish front fenders that flowed into a curved rear fenderline. The trunk deck had large, canted taillights that blended into the rear fenders.

Rambler started the '60s with a choice of two engines, a six and a V-8. The six, a holdover from Nash days, displaced 195.6 cubic inches and developed 127 or 138 hp. It was standard on Classics through 1964. The V-8 had been designed for use by Hudson and Nash in the mid-1950s. In 1960-61 Rambler form, it displaced 250 cubic inches (bore and stroke 3.50 x 3.25 inches) and developed either 200 or 215 hp.

The 1961 Classic V-8 scored well in both performance and economy. When equipped with the optional Flashomatic (Borg-Warner) automatic transmission, it could spring from 0 to 60 mph in ten seconds, and deliver 16 to 20 miles per gallon. But the V-8 was heavier than the six, and gave Ramblers pronounced understeer. No less than 57 percent of the V-8 model's weight was positioned over its front wheels. Sales of the V-8 were not high. When the Ambassador was made smaller for 1962-63, the V-8 Classic was temporarily dropped.

In 1964 the Classic V-8 returned to the line with a 287-cid engine (3.75 x 3.25) and 198 hp. In 1965, a 270-hp version was available. For the 1967 Rambler Rebel, the engine was stroked to 290 cubic inches, to deliver 200 hp. A larger V-8, the Ambassador 327 with 250 to 270 hp, was offered on Rambler Classics for 1966. For the 1967 Rambler Rebel, it was enlarged by boring and stroking to 343 cid, which gave it 235 or 280 hp, depending on its state of tune.

As an option to 1964's standard six, Rambler brought out a new oversquare engine, the Torque Command six, which displaced 232 cubic inches (3.75 x 3.50) and yielded 145 hp. About 2,500 special Rambler Typhoon hardtops, painted yellow and black, were released to celebrate the occasion. The Torque Command engine was optional on Classics and Rebels through 1967, with a 155-hp alternative from 1965 through 1968.

At the lower end of the AMC scale was the Rambler American. This 100-inch-wheelbase compact had been dropped in 1956, but was reinstated in 1958 when the economy-car boom started. In 1960 form, the American was an anachronism. It had the old Pininfarina-styled body and an ancient Nash L-head six of 195.6 cid and 90 hp. Deluxe, Super and Custom models were offered in sedan and wagon form, with

1962 Rambler American Super Four-Door Station Wagon

1963 Rambler Ambassador 990 Two-Door Sedan

1964 Rambler American 440-H Two-Door Hardtop

prices beginning at $1,795. Convinced that the American was marketable, AMC restyled it in 1961 and gave it a new engine.

The overhead-valve 1961 American engine had actually appeared in mid-1960. Formerly, it had been reserved for the larger Ramblers. Available on Americans with either 90 or 127 hp, it provided fuel mileage in the middle 20s, plus an adequate performance. The '61 body style, created by Edmund Anderson, was something else again. It was boxy and truncated, and had odd, concave body sculpture. Sedans, business coupes, two-door and four-door wagons, and a convertible were offered in three series. Although they were genuine economy cars and provided a fair amount of interior room, they were anything but beautiful. Teague decided to change them at all costs for 1964.

Teague's new American had a longer, 106-inch wheelbase, since the Rambler Classic had already gone from 108 to 112. It was a clean design having curved glass and modest brightwork—quite in keeping with its function. The styling was so good, in fact, that it wasn't significantly altered for the rest of the decade. By 1968 the American and American-based Rogue hardtop were the only AMC cars bearing the Rambler

Rambler

1965 Rambler Classic 770 Convertible

1965 Rambler Marlin

1966 Rambler American 440 Convertible

1967 Rambler Rebel SST Two-Door Hardtop

1967 Rambler Rogue Convertible

name. They were all sixes, offering 128 to 145 horsepower.

In 1969, Rambler's last year as a make, an identical lineup of Americans and Rogues was launched. An American could still be bought for less than $2,000. A post-introduction decision was to offer AMC's new 290-cid, 200-hp V-8 in the American as an option. This led to a limited-edition Rogue equipped with an even-larger 390-cid engine that produced 315 hp, a Hurst shifter, and the designation SC/Rambler. These "Scramblers" were sold for $2,998 each to a handful of buyers. They weren't in keeping with the traditional Rambler image, but were impressive performers.

Teague hastily conjured up a bucket-seated fastback for 1965, to do battle with the Mustang and Barracuda. The result was the Marlin, a Rambler model in 1965 and a make in its own right thereafter. The Marlin was basically a Rambler Classic, reworked above the beltline with a huge glassed-in roof. The 232 six and 327 V-8 were offered. When equipped with the V-8, a Marlin would do 0 to 60 in 12 seconds and the standing quarter mile in 18 seconds at 76 mph. That wasn't earthshaking, but it was performance of a sort. And that had been the goal: turn the public image of Rambler around, making the cars appear sporty and fun to drive instead of dull and economical. But the Marlin didn't sell. Only 10,327 copies of the '65 edition were produced.

The origin of the big Ambassador can be traced back to prewar years, and on through 1957 when it had been a Nash model. From 1958 through 1965 it was a Rambler model; from 1966 on it was an individual make. Ambassador sales were never high, but AMC's management kept the car in the lineup to fill any gaps that might develop as a result of changing public taste.

The 117-inch-wheelbase 1958 Ambassador had at first been slated as a Hudson and Nash model. Ultimately, AMC's managers saw no value in those names, so they dubbed it a Rambler. The 1960-61 versions were continuations of the original '58. They had luxurious interiors and excessive ornamentation. The three series were priced from $2,400 to about $3,200. The price leader in both years was the Deluxe four-door sedan. In addition there were Super and Custom four-doors, and wagons with either six or eight seats. In 1961, a posh Custom 400 sedan with the highest-quality trim, standard automatic, and a $2,814 price was added to the Ambassador series. Ambassadors came with the 327-cid V-8, which produced 250 hp in standard form or 270 with four-barrel carburetor.

By the end of the decade, AMC's managers had decided that the large Ambassador V-8s were not saleable. For 1962, therefore, the 117-inch wheelbase was dropped, and the Ambassadors shared the Classic's body. The optional V-8 was dropped from the Classic series; the Ambassadors were available only with the 327 V-8.

For 1963 Teague planned to restyle the Classic. That, of course, meant a restyled Ambassador as well. Again, both cars shared the same wheelbase of 112 inches. The Ambassador was the V-8 model.

1968 Rambler American 440 Station Wagon

1969 Rambler 440 Four-Door Sedan

1968 Rambler Rogue Hardtop

1969 Rambler Rogue Hardtop

From a distance, Classics and Ambassadors looked almost identical—and they were similar, except for their power plants. For 1964 the Classic was made available with a small V-8 option. The Ambassador was then restricted to one, 327-powered 990 series. There was a sedan, a Cross Country wagon, and two hardtop coupes called the 990 and 990H. The 990H was the only Ambassador available with the 270-hp engine.

The 1964 lineup wasn't particularly successful, so by 1965 the game plan was changed again. The Ambassador got its own 116-inch wheelbase; the Classic stayed with the 112. Ambassadors could be ordered with the 232-cid six. The standard V-8 was the 287-cid unit. The 327, of 270-hp, was an option. There were almost no changes for 1966, but the Ambassador was then registered as a separate make.

The styling of the Rambler Ambassador for 1965 was probably the best it had ever been. Teague's foursquare design resulted in an intermediate-size car that was comparable with the Ford Fairlane, but that had distinctive looks and more interior space. The models were the 880 two-door and four-door sedan and wagon; the luxury 990 four-door sedan, wagon, and hardtop, and the 990H hardtop and convertible. AMC made a play for the soft-top market in 1965; there was a convertible in every line—American, Classic and Ambassador.

The convertibles leaked when the curved side windows were opened, and they did not sell well. Production of the soft-top models in 1965 consisted of 3,882 Americans, 4,953 Classics, and 3,499 Ambassadors. The Ambassador convertible was dropped after 1967.

	1960	1961	1962	1963	1964	1965	1966	1967	1968	1969
RAMBLER AT A GLANCE, 1960-1969										
Price Range, $	1781-3151	1833-3113	1832-3471	1832-3018	1907-2985	1979-3063	2017-2629	2073-2872	1946-2426	1998-2998
Weight Range, lbs.	2428-3592	2454-3566	2454-3023	2446-3305	2506-3350	2492-3388	2554-3071	2591-3288	2604-2800	2604-3160
Wheelbases, in.	100-117	100-117	100-108	100-112	106-112	106-116	106-112	106-114	106	106
6 Cyl. Engines, hp	90-138	90-138	90-138	90-138	90-145	90-155	128-155	128-155	128-155	128-145
8 Cyl. Engines, hp	200-270	200-270	250-270	198-270	198-270	198-270	198-270	200-280	200-225	200-315

Shelby

**Shelby Automotive, Ionia, Michigan;
Ford Motor Co., Dearborn, Michigan**

Carroll Shelby, who retired from racing for health reasons in 1960, settled down to become America's most charismatic manufacturer of specialty cars. Between 1962 and 1970 he built or contributed to many blindingly fast, race-worthy classics: the AC Cobra, Sunbeam Tiger, Cobra 427, Ford GT40, and Ford Mark IV. He helped bring Ford to its racing pinnacle, the winning of Le Mans.

Shelby's most popular project, from the standpoint of sales, was the GT-350, a super-tuned version of the Ford Mustang. Built by Shelby Automotive in 1965-66, it was an uncompromisingly potent grand touring car, equally at home on road or track. Later Shelbys, built by Ford from 1967 through 1970, were not quite the cars their predecessors had been; but they were good examples of what talented specialists could do with a basically good package like the Mustang.

The 1965 GT-350 was aimed primarily at the B-production racing class of the Sports Car Club of America. (It was B-production champion in 1965-67.) Shelby took a blue-striped white Mustang fastback and installed the high performance version of Ford's 289 cubic-inch V-8 in it. Then he added a high-rise manifold, a big four-barrel carburetor, and free-flow exhaust headers. This brought horsepower up to 306 at 6000 rpm. All Shelbys came with a Borg-Warner T10 four-speed gearbox, a regular Mustang option. Instead of the Mustang's Falcon-based rear axle, GT-350s used a stronger unit from the Fairlane station wagon. Other significant components included metallic-lined rear brakes, Koni shock absorbers, and disc front brakes with metallic pads. Steering was made quicker by relocating the front suspension mounting points. And by connecting the tops of the front shock absorbers to each other with a length of steel tubing, Shelby prevented shock flex under hard cornering. The result of his chassis tuning was nearly neutral handling, instead of the stock Mustang's strong understeer.

Shelby cast his own 15-inch aluminum wheels and

shod them with high-performance Goodyear bias-ply tires. He replaced the stock Mustang hood with one made of fiberglass. It contained a prominent scoop and was held down by NASCAR hood pins. Shelby also removed the prancing horse from the grille, and made Mustang's fake side scoops functional to cool the rear brakes. For 1966, the fastback's stock air-exit grilles in the rear of the roof were replaced by plastic quarter windows.

Shelby's only changes to the Mustang's interior consisted of the installation of competition-style three-inch seat belts and a mahogany-rimmed steering wheel. GT-350s came with the rear seat removed and the spare tire lashed down in the vacated space. Strangely, Shelby offered a kit so the buyer could put the spare back in the trunk and install a new rear seat. The stock front seats were left alone. All the interiors were black.

In the racing version of the GT-350, Shelby achieved 350 hp—an astounding 1.21 horsepower per cubic inch. The engine used in this car was basically the same as that of the racing Cobra 289. Its four-speed gearbox had an aluminum case to cut weight. The interior was stripped and a racing seat was installed, along with a roll bar and safety harness. Competition tires and an ultra-heavy suspension were installed. A special fiberglass nose eliminated the front bumper and provided a rudimentary air dam. It had a central slot for cooling air. The ultimate racing GT-350 had four-wheel disc brakes, a 400-hp engine, and wide tires under flared fenders.

Hertz Rent-A-Car got into the act in 1966 when it ordered 936 Shelbys, painted black with gold stripes. Hertz called this car the GT-350H, and would rent one for $17 a day and 17 cents a mile. The Hertz model was a stock GT-350, aside from the paint job and the company's use of a three-speed automatic transmission instead of a four-speed manual. Hertz rented some of its GT-350Hs to weekend racers, and a few of

1965 Shelby GT-350 Fastback

1968 Shelby GT-500 Fastback

1968 Shelby GT-500 Convertible

them performed successfully on SCCA tracks.

In 1967 Ford Motor Company built a larger, heavier Mustang and offered it with the big-block 390-cid V-8. Shelby did Ford one better and tossed in a huge 428-cid V-8. He called the result the GT-500. It was sold as a linemate to the GT-350. Shelby advertised the GT-500 at 335 hp, but the car probably had closer to 400 horses. The GT-350 for 1967 was advertised at its usual 306 hp, but the real figure was below 300 because the '67 did not have the steel-tube exhaust headers of the '66 model.

The '67s had their own fiberglass front end, distinctive from the Mustang's, and other styling modifications, but only small chassis refinements. They also bore a new emblem: a coiled cobra in anodized gold. The interior featured a huge, black-painted roll bar, to which were affixed inertia-reel seat belts instead of the three-inch harness type of 1966. Over 3,000 of the 1967s were built, and were sold at lower prices than the 1965-66 models.

In 1968 the 350 and 500 models were offered again, their front ends having been fitted with a wider hood scoop than before. Their interiors were from the Mustang. A Stewart Warner oil pressure gauge and ammeter were mounted on the center console. A convertible was added to each line, priced about $100 higher than the comparable fastback. Also new was the GT-500KR ("King of the Road"), which had Ford's Cobra Jet 428 block, extra-large heads and intake manifold, and a Holley 735 cfm four-barrel carburetor. The KR sold for $4,472 as a fastback, and $4,692 as a convertible.

Mechanically the 1969 GT-350 and GT-500 were more closely related to the Mustangs than their predecessors had been. (The Mustang was all-new that year.) Their fiberglass front fenders contained air scoops, and their side stripes were located midway up the bodysides. The GT-350s were powered by the new 351-cid engine, which developed 290 hp; the GT-500s used the 428-cid Cobra Jet engine, rated at 335 hp.

Although a few of the 1969s were reserialized for 1970, Shelby production effectively ended in '69. A combination of government regulations and spiraling insurance rates for the cars (their accident record was staggering) prompted Carroll Shelby to ask the then-president of Ford, Lee Iacocca, to cancel the program.

SHELBY AT A GLANCE, 1960-1969

	1960	1961	1962	1963	1964	1965	1966	1967	1968	1969
Price Range, $						4547	4600	3995-4195	4117-4692	4434-5027
Weight Range, lbs.						2800	2800	2800-3000	2900-3100	2900-3100
Wheelbases, in.						108	108	108	108	108
8 Cyl. Engines, hp						306-400	306-400	290-400	250-400+	290-335

Studebaker
Studebaker Corp.
South Bend, Indiana; Hamilton, Ontario

America's oldest car producer met its end in 1966, after a series of disasters, rescue attempts, and relapses.

Studebaker's troubles began in the Great Depression, when the company slipped into receivership. The firm pulled itself together with the 1939 Champion, then set records in the postwar seller's market. But its luck didn't hold. Marketing miscalculations, quality-control problems, a disintegrating dealer force, and diminished public confidence brought Studebaker to the brink of extinction once in 1956 and again in 1958.

A reprieve arrived in the form of the 1959 Lark—a truncated version of a '50s sedan. The Lark made its debut exactly on time, during the economy-car swing of the late 1950s. This car brought Studebaker its first profit in five years. But the company's failure to substantially update and improve the Lark in the '60s caused sales to decline again. The firm's other interesting models could not stop its downward slide. A succession of presidents—Harold Churchill, Clarence Francis, Sherwood Egbert, and Byers Burlingame—conducted a succession of rescue programs until the company's financial backers gave up.

The Lark for 1960 was changed only mildly from the introductory 1959 model. It got a new grille composed of thick and thin horizontal bars, and small alterations in script and medallions. The sedan wheelbase was 108.5 inches; the station wagon's was 113 inches. The Lark VI was an old, long-stroke 169.6-cid L-head (3.0 x 4.0 inches) that developed 90 hp. It was used in the Deluxe two-door and four-door sedans, the Regal four-door sedan and hardtop coupe; and three different station wagons. The Lark VIII engine (the origins of which can be traced back to 1951) displaced 259 cubic inches (3.56 x 3.25) and developed 180 hp in standard form, with 195 hp optional. It was available in the same combination of Deluxes and Regals as the six, plus a pretty two-door convertible. Eight-cylinder power plants were priced about $280 higher than sixes.

The company continued to build its specialty Hawk in 1960. Like the Lark, it was only slightly altered from 1959. The Hawk, a five-window coupe, stemmed from the 1953 Starlight created by the Raymond Loewy studios. Since 1956 it had featured a classic-style square grille. And since '57 it had had large concave tail fins. Its wheelbase was 120.5 inches; its engine was a V-8 that displaced 289 cubic inches and produced 210 hp. The Hawk sold for $2,650, and was worth it. Equipped with functional white-on-black instruments and semi-bucket seats, and offering good performance, the Hawk was a unique "family sports car." Unfortunately, a dearth of dealerships and advertising, plus emphasis on the Lark, hampered sales. Only 3,719 Hawks were built for 1960.

The 1961 Larks were little different from the 1960s. The six-cylinder engine, however, was converted to overhead-valve design. In this form, it provided 112 hp. One new model was the Lark Cruiser, which rode the

1960 Studebaker Hawk

1962 Studebaker Gran Turismo Hawk (prototype)

1960 Studebaker Lark Regal Convertible

1963 Studebaker GT "White Hawk" show car

wagon wheelbase. It was outfitted with rich upholstery and was designed for extra rear seat room. Cruisers could be ordered with the Hawk 289 V-8, which was available with a power pack consisting of a four-barrel carburetor and dual exhausts that raised output to 225 hp. The Hawk was slightly revised for 1961. It was given two-tone color panels just below the fins on the rear fenders and an optional four-speed gearbox. Studebaker built 3,117 of the 1961 Hawks.

When Sherwood Egbert became company president in early 1961, he asked the Milwaukee stylist Brooks Stevens to help redesign the Lark and Hawk on a six-month crash program. Randall Faurot, Studebaker's head of styling, willing stepped back and let Stevens direct the effort. Stevens adopted the 113-inch wheelbase for all four-door models. He also developed elongated rear quarters, large round taillights, and a Mercedes-like grille (Studebaker was distributing Mercedes-Benz cars at the time). A deluxe model available with both the six and the V-8 was the sporty Lark Daytona, which had bucket seats, bright new interiors, and an optional 289 engine.

In reworking the Hawk, Stevens reskinned the old Loewy coupe to create a hardtop instead of a pillared model. He eliminated the large Hawk tail fins, which had become dated by 1962. Stevens gave the car a unique dashboard that contained a purposeful bank of instruments that were canted toward the driver. This Gran Turismo Hawk was a remarkable piece of expeditious redesign. Its optional 225-hp engine made it fly. A top speed of 120 mph and a 0 to 60 sprint in less than 10 seconds were possible. Although heavy, the 289 was incredibly strong and capable of performance far greater than its displacement suggests. Sales picked up in 1962—nearly 8,000 Gran Turismos were built. In calendar year production, Studebaker jumped from 79,000 units in '61 to 87,000 in '62. This would be its only gain of the decade.

For 1963, Brooks Stevens redesigned the Lark body above the beltline. He improved visibility by using a large glass area and thin upper door frames. The grille was revised slightly. The dashboard was completely new. It had comprehensive needle gauges, rocker-type control switches, and a "vanity" style glove compartment, which contained a makeup case and pop-up mirror. For utility-car buyers, Stevens came up with a great innovation: the Wagonaire, with sliding rear roof.

Stevens gave the 1963 GT Hawk a new grille similar to the Lark's, round amber parking lights, a wood-like dash, and pleated vinyl seats. Both the Lark and the Hawk were available by mid-year with the R1 (240 hp) and R2 (335 hp) Avanti engines, options priced at $372 and $210. The R2 Super Hawk exceeded 140 mph at Bonneville, and an R2 Super Lark did over 132 mph.

Yet Studebaker sales plunged in 1963. Calendar year output fell short of 68,000 units. The company ranked 12th in production, ahead of only Lincoln and Imperial among the major makes. Egbert, who'd been hospitalized repeatedly, entered the hospital again in November 1963, and did not return to the company. (He died of cancer in 1969.) Byers Burlingame

replaced him as president. A month later, after desperate last-ditch attempts to obtain backing for future models, Burlingame announced the closure of Studebaker's South Bend factory. Manufacture was removed to the assembly plant in Hamilton, Ontario. Managers there hoped to continue building Studebakers at the rate of 20,000 a year. After '64, all Studebakers were Canadian-built.

The 1964 models were the most attractive Studebakers of the decade. Brooks Stevens had created more new styling for the Cruiser, Daytona, and Lark. This consisted of a crisp, squared-off body, six inches

1963 Studebaker Lark Daytona Wagonaire Station Wagon

1964 Studebaker Commander Four-Door Sedan

1965 Studebaker Daytona Two-Door Sedan

1966 Studebaker Cruiser Four-Door Sedan

Brooks Stevens' styling study for proposed 1966 Studebaker Sceptre

Studebaker

longer than that of the 1963 models; a broad, horizontal grille integrated with the headlights; and a pointed upper tail section for the back-up lights and taillamps. A stripped Challenger line had been added at around $2,000, and a still-more-powerful R3 engine was announced for the Super Lark and Super Hawk. (The Super Lark could do 0 to 60 in 7.3 seconds.) The 1964 GT Hawk had a landau-style roof with partial vinyl top (optional), a smoothed-off deck, and a matte-black dash instead of a woodgrain one. A test driver pushed an R2 Hawk to 90 mph in 13.8 seconds and estimated its top speed at 150-plus mph. These special models were dropped after production moved to Canada. Production of GT Hawks had never picked up. Only 3,649 of them were built for 1963, and just 1,484 for 1964. Studebaker's overall sales also were dismal: fewer than 20,000 units were sold in calendar 1964. The 1965 Studebakers were unchanged in styling.

However, since Studebaker's South Bend engine plant had closed, the Hamilton factory had to use new engines. Its source was Chevrolet. Chevy provided its solid 194-cid six, which developed 120 hp, and its excellent 283-cid V-8 of 195 hp. A Cruiser powered by the six was available. Other six-cylinder models were the Commander two-door and four-door sedan, and four-door Wagonaire (with or without sliding roof). The V-8 powered the Commander sedans and wagon, a Daytona hardtop and wagon, and a Cruiser.

The Hamilton plant almost did produce its 20,000-unit quota for 1965. But the lack of any facilities for advance research and development meant that production simply couldn't last. The 1966 Studebakers, which had new front end styling—two dual-beam headlights instead of quads, a new grille with rectangular panels, new body side molding, and a rear panel with air-extraction ports—numbered only 8,447 units. Despite rescue attempts by Stevens and others, Studebaker was doomed. Its range of prototypes (from economy cars to a revived Packard) never saw production.

STUDEBAKER AT A GLANCE, 1960-1969										
	1960	1961	1962	1963	1964	1965	1966	1967	1968	1969
Price Range, $	1976-2756	1935-2689	1935-3080	1935-2650	1943-2966	2125-2890	2125-2890			
Weight Range, lbs.	2588-3315	2661-3315	2655-3305	2650-3490	2660-3555	2695-3505	2680-3490			
Wheelbases, in.	108.5-120.5	108.5-120.5	109-120.5	109-120.5	109-120.5	109-113	109-113			
6 Cyl. Engines, hp	90	112	112	112	112	120	120			
8 Cyl. Engines, hp	180-210	180-225	180-225	180-335	180-290	195	195			

Studebaker Avanti
Studebaker Corp.
South Bend, Indiana

The Avanti was a brilliantly conceived grand touring car created by Raymond Loewy and a team of talented designers—John Ebstein, Robert Andrews, and Tom Kellogg. Loewy had been hired by Studebaker's president, Sherwood Egbert, who wanted an exotic sports-type car that would revitalize his company's image. Egbert asked for a four-seater with aerodynamic lines.

Creation of the Avanti was the first assignment Loewy had received from Studebaker since his old contract lapsed after the design of the 1956 Hawks. In haste and complete secrecy, he gathered his team at a rented house in Palm Springs, California.

The car Loewy developed had a Coke-bottle shape, a large rear window, and a built-in roll bar. The front fenders were razor-edged. They swept back into curved rear fenders and a jacked-up duck-like tail. Avoiding a conventional grille, Loewy designed an air scoop under the thin front bumper. An asymmetrical hump was built into the hood to direct the driver's vision and add character to the shape of the car. Inside, ample crash padding was used, together with four slim-section vinyl bucket seats and complete instrumentation. The design was accepted for production with very little change from Loewy's original quarter-scale model.

Fiberglass was chosen as the body material for reasons of cost and time. Studebaker's chief engineer Eugene Hardig used a Lark convertible frame for the Avanti body. The frame was shortened and highly modified. It had special front and rear anti-sway bars, and rear radius rods. Bendix disc brakes were used on the Avanti (as well as on some Studebaker Larks and Hawks). They were the first caliper discs in domestic production. The Avanti engine was, of course, the 289 V-8. In standard ("R1") form, it developed 240 hp, thanks to its Paxton supercharger, ¾ race high-lift cam, dual-breaker distributor, four-barrel carburetor, and dual exhaust. Andy Granatelli and Paxton also developed a supercharged R2 version, which had 290 hp. This was followed by a bored-out 304.5-cid V-8 in

1964 Studebaker Avanti

three higher states of tune, the R3, R4, and R5. The supercharged R3 had 9.6:1 compression and developed 335 hp. The R4 was unblown, but it used two four-barrel carbs and had 12:1 compression, and thus developed 280 hp. The experimental R5 was astounding. It had two Paxton superchargers, one for each cylinder bank, along with magneto ignition and Bendix fuel injection. It developed an incredible 575 horsepower.

The Avanti had a remarkably slippery shape, even though Loewy had not had time for wind-tunnel tests—he'd just guessed. It was a natural for high-speed trials. In late 1962 with an R3, Andy Granatelli broke 29 Bonneville speed records, traveling faster than anyone had ever run an American stock car.

Unfortunately, Studebaker failed to get the Avanti into volume production immediately after announcement. Unexpected distortion occurred during fiberglass curing and this delayed body production. As a result, Studebaker was forced to add its own fiberglass facility. By the time all the bugs were out, most of the customers who'd placed advance orders had given up on the Avanti and had bought Corvettes. Fewer than 4,600 Avantis were produced during 1963 and 1964. Avanti production had already ceased by the time Studebaker stopped building Larks in December 1963.

The car was revived, however, by a pair of South Bend dealers. Equipped with a Corvette engine, it's still in production today. (See the Avanti II chapter.)

STUDEBAKER AVANTI AT A GLANCE, 1960-1969										
	1960	1961	1962	1963	1964	1965	1966	1967	1968	1969
Price Range, $				4445	4445					
Weight Range, lbs.				3140	3195					
Wheelbases, in.				109	109					
8 Cyl. Engines, hp				240-335	240-335					

Model Year Production Chart

Automotive production figures can be confusing, because car makers and industry observers sometimes discuss production in terms of model years and calendar years. The two are not the same; each firm builds cars of two different model years between January 1 and December 31 of a single calendar year.

The following chart lists production figures for model years rather than calendar years unless otherwise specified. (Most of the figures discussed in the text of the *Cars of the 60s* are calendar-year figures.)

	1960	1961	1962	1963	1964	1965	1966	1967	1968	1969
AMERICAN MOTORS										
Ambassador							71,692	62,615	54,641	75,741
AMX									6,725	8,293
Javelin									56,462	40,675
Marlin							4,547	2,545		
Rebel									69,607	48,397
AVANTI II						21	77	60	84	103
BUICK										
Special		74,185	110,870	106,449	98,762	101,601	103,097	86,041	49,475	35,648
Skylark		12,683	42,973	42,321	85,870	133,368	106,217	107,292	178,025	152,695
LeSabre	152,082	113,230	127,198	171,183	135,163	144,996	142,399	155,190	179,748	197,866
Invicta	45,411	28,733	56,017	3,495						
Wildcat				35,725	82,245	98,787	68,584	70,881	69,969	67,453
Riviera				40,000	37,658	34,586	45,348	42,799	49,284	52,872
Electra	56,314	47,923	62,468	58,665	68,792	86,807	88,225	100,304	125,362	158,618
CADILLAC										
Series 62	70,842	62,426	70,277	64,298	52,979					
Calais						34,211	28,680	21,830	18,190	12,425
De Ville	53,389	55,174	55,653	79,049	92,496	123,080	142,190	139,807	164,472	163,048
Eldorado	2,443	1,450	1,450	1,825	1,870	2,125	2,250	17,930	24,528	23,333
60 Special	11,800	15,500	13,350	14,000	14,550	18,100	19,075	16,300	18,600	19,845
Series 75	1,550	1,625	1,600	1,475	1,425	1,250	2,017	1,800	1,800	2,036
Comm. Chassis	2,160	2,204	2,280	2,527	2,639	2,669	2,463	2,333	2,413	2,550
CHECKER ■	6,980	5,683	8,173	7,050	6,310	6,136	5,761	5,822	5,477	5,417
CHEVROLET▲										
Biscayne	287,700	204,000	166,000	186,500	173,900	145,300	122,400	92,800	82,100	68,700
Bel Air	381,500	330,000	365,500	354,100	318,100	271,400	236,600	179,700	152,200	155,700
Impala	511,900	491,000	704,900	832,600	889,600	803,400	654,900	575,600	710,900	777,000
Wagon	212,700	(inc. above)	187,600	198,500	192,800	184,400	185,500	155,100	175,600	(inc. above)
Chevy II			326,600	375,600	191,700	122,100	163,300	106,500	201,000	270,000
Chevelle					328,400	344,100	412,000	369,100	422,900	439,600
Impala SS						243,100	119,300	74,000		
Caprice							181,000	124,500	115,500	166,900
Camaro								220,900	235,100	243,100

■ (Calendar year, includes taxicabs)

▲ (Chevrolet production rounded to nearest 100)

	1960	1961	1962	1963	1964	1965	1966	1967	1968	1969
CHEV. CORVAIR										
500	62,311	41,200	16,245	16,680	22,968	54,307	32,824	12,216	7,206	2,762
700	175,770	97,185	57,558	33,062	16,295					
Monza	11,926	143,690	209,560	185,730	140,781	152,557	60,447	15,037	8,193	3,238
Monza Spyder			9,468	19,099	11,441					
Corsa						28,654	10,472			
CHEV. CORVETTE										
Convertible	10,261	10,939	14,531	10,919	13,925	15,376	17,762	14,436	18,630	16,608
Coupe				10,594	8,304	8,186	9,958	8,504	9,936	22,154
CHRYSLER										
Windsor	41,158	17,336								
Saratoga	15,525									
Newport		57,102	83,120	75,972	85,183	125,795	167,711	157,371	182,099	156,836
"300"			25,020	24,665	25,318	27,678	49,597	21,888	34,621	32,472
New Yorker	19,390	20,399	20,223	27,960	31,044	49,871	47,579	39,457	48,143	46,947
300F to 300L	1,212	1,617	558	400	3,647	2,845				
Town & Country □										24,516
CONTINENTAL										
Mark V	11,086									
Mark III									7,770	23,088
DESOTO										
Fireflite	14,484									
Adventurer	11,597									
(standard)		3,034								
DODGE (U.S. & CANADA)										
Lancer		74,774	64,271							
Dart	323,168	180,561	146,360	153,922	192,673	209,376	176,027	154,495	171,772	197,685
Matador	27,908									
330/440				148,100	188,403					
880			17,505	28,266	31,760	44,496				
Polara	16,728	14,032	12,268	7,256	88,585	109,811	107,832	76,464	106,687	91,721
Coronet						209,392	250,842	183,802	220,831	203,425
Monaco						13,096	60,613	40,462	41,980	38,566
Charger							37,344	15,788	96,108	89,700
EDSEL										
Ranger	2,571									
Villager	275									
EXCALIBUR (totals only)										
SSK										168
Roadster (1966-1969)										59
Phaeton (1966-69)										89
FORD										
Falcon	435,676	474,241	414,282	328,339	300,770	213,601	182,669	64,335	131,389	96,016
Custom/300/500	874	352		70,152	188,770	236,757	243,775	160,930	122,846	114,438
Fairlane	204,793	163,477	79,606	97,444	47,114	52,974	83,431	65,499	102,592	123,808
Fairlane 500	244,275	141,385	217,510	246,443	230,472	170,980	233,643	173,189	114,425	114,049
Galaxie/500XL	289,268	349,665	170,524	112,754					56,114	61,959
Galaxie 500			404,600	535,256	593,533	457,129	495,904	426,941	339,262	311,388
station wagon	171,824	136,619	129,654	127,130	140,929	177,664	195,153	178,751	208,318	238,523
LTD (Galaxie model, 1965-66)						105,729	101,096	110,505	138,752	288,442
Torino (Fairlane model) △									157,310	129,058

□ (from 1960 through 1968: included under individual series above.)

△ **Note:** Falcon, Fairlane & Torino include wagons; Falcon Econoline & Club Wagon not included

	1960	1961	1962	1963	1964	1965	1966	1967	1968	1969
FORD MUSTANG										
fastback						77,079	35,698	71,042	42,581	61,980
hardtop						501,965	499,751	356,271	249,447	128,458
convertible						101,945	72,119	44,808	25,376	14,746
Mach I										72,458
Grande										22,182
FORD THUNDERBIRD										
hardtop	80,983	62,535	68,127	42,806	60,552	42,652	29,022	15,567	9,977	5,913
convertible	11,860	10,516	8,457	5,913	9,198	6,846	5,049			
Sports Roadster			1,427	455						
Landau, 2 dr.				14,139	22,715	25,474	35,105	37,422	33,029	27,664
Landau, 4 dr.								24,967	21,925	15,695
IMPERIAL										
Custom/Standard	7,786	5,018	4,413	4,013				2,193	1,887	
Crown	8,226	6,205	8,475	8,558	20,336	16,235	11,864	13,227	12,622	2,684
Le Baron	1,691	1,026	1,449	1,537	2,949	2,164	1,878	2,194	1,852	19,393
Crown Imperial	16	9	0	13	10	10	10			
Le Baron limousine						estimated:		6	6	6
LINCOLN										
standard	7,160									
Premiere	6,574									
Continental sedan		22,307	27,849	28,095	32,969	36,824	35,809	32,331	29,719	29,258
Continental convert.		2,857	3,212	3,138	3,328	3,356	3,180	2,276		
Continental coupe							15,766	11,060	9,415	9,032
MERCURY										
Comet & Montego	116,331	197,263	165,305	134,623	189,936	165,052	170,426	81,133	123,113	117,421
Meteor/S-55			53,122	69,052	50,775		3,585			
Monterey	102,539	50,128	89,024	107,072	42,587	80,373	65,688	49,398	57,014	53,065
Montclair	19,814				32,963	45,546	38,913	19,922	14,760	
Park Lane	10,287				19,611	32,405	38,800	20,476	14,803	
station wagon▲	22,360	16,838	17,985	13,976	15,181	23,375	25,741	26,588	29,867	33,368
Cougar								150,893	113,726	100,069
Marquis								6,510	3,965	43,436
Brougham									5,691	37,962
Marauder										14,666
METROPOLITAN										
1500○	13,103	853	412							

▲(Note: "station wagon" covers full-size wagons only.)
○(Shipments from U.K.)

1960 Imperial Le Baron Four-Door Southampton

1967 Oldsmobile Toronado

	1960	1961	1962	1963	1964	1965	1966	1967	1968	1969
OLDSMOBILE										
F-85/Cutlass		76,394	94,568	118,811	177,618	212,870	229,573	251,461	275,128	239,289
Dynamic 88	189,864	138,380	188,737	199,315	167,674	119,497	95,834			
Super 88	97,913	53,164	58,147	62,770	37,514					
Jetstar/Delmont 88					78,589	61,989	30,247	108,356	121,418	
Delta 88						90,467	88,626	88,096	102,505	252,087
Ninety Eight	59,364	43,012	64,154	70,308	68,554	92,406	88,494	76,539	92,072	116,783
Starfire		7,600	41,988	25,549	16,163	15,260	13,019			
Toronado							40,963	21,790	26,521	28,520
PLYMOUTH	483,969	356,257	339,527	488,448	551,633	728,228	687,514	638,075	790,239	751,134
PONTIAC										
Tempest		100,783	143,193	131,490	226,577	231,731	262,152	184,738	258,722	215,628
GTO					32,450	75,352	96,946	81,722	87,684	72,287
Catalina	210,934	113,354	204,654	234,549	257,768	271,058	254,310	240,750	276,182	246,596
Ventura	56,277	27,209								
Starchief/Executive	43,691	29,581	41,642	40,757	37,653	31,315	45,212	46,987	44,635	39,061
Bonneville	85,277	69,323	101,753	109,539	120,259	134,020	135,401	102,996	104,436	96,315
Firebird								82,560	107,112	87,708
Grand Prix			30,195	72,959	63,810	57,881	36,757	42,981	31,711	112,486
RAMBLER										
(Total registrations)	422,273	370,685	423,104	428,346	379,412	324,669	265,712	237,785	259,346	239,937
SHELBY										
GT-350						562	2,378	1,175	1,648	1,279
GT-500								2,050	1,557	1,871
GT-500KR									1,246	
STUDEBAKER										
2-dr. sedan	30,453	13,275	17,636	15,726	5,485	7,372	2,321			
4-dr. sedan	48,382	28,670	41,894	30,795	15,908	10,239	5,686			
2-dr. hardtop	6,867	3,211	7,888	3,259	1,734					
2-dr. wagon	4,833	2,166								
4-dr. wagon	17,902	6,552	9,687	10,487	3,702	1,824	440			
convertible	8,306	1,898	2,599	773	411					
Hawk	3,719	3,117	7,842	3,649	1,484					
taxi & chassis	3	824	1,772	1,121	450					
STUDEBAKER AVANTI										
coupe				3,744	795					

1961 Plymouth Fury Two-Door Hardtop

1963 Studebaker Avanti

Sources

The following books are the standard works on their subjects. They all provide comprehensive information about makes discussed in *Cars of the '60s*. Most titles are available from Classic Motorbooks, Box 2, Osceola, WI 54020, or from your local bookstore.

Avanti II
Bonsall, Thomas, *Avanti*.

Buick
Dunne, Jim; Norbye, Jan P., *Buick, The Postwar Years*.

Cadillac
Hendry, Maurice, *Cadillac, The Complete History*.

Chevrolet
Dammann, George, *Sixty Years of Chevrolet*.
Given, Kyle, *Corvair, A History*.
Ludvigsen, Karl E., *Corvette, America's Star-Spangled Sports Car*.

Chrysler
Langworth, Richard M., *Chrysler and Imperial, The Postwar Years*.

DeSoto
Butler, Don, *The Plymouth-DeSoto Story*.

Dodge
MacPherson, Thomas A., *The Dodge Story*.

Edsel
Deutsch, Jan, *Selling the People's Cadillac*.

Ford
Dammann, George H., *Illustrated History of Ford*.

Imperial
Langworth, Richard M., *Chrysler and Imperial, The Postwar Years*.

Plymouth
Butler, Don, *The Plymouth-DeSoto Story*.

Pontiac
Dunne, Jim; Norbye, Jan P., *Pontiac, The Postwar Years*.

Shelby
Kopec, Rick, *The Shelby-American Guide*.

Studebaker
Langworth, Richard M., *Studebaker, The Postwar Years*.

1967 AMC Marlin

1968 Buick Electra 225 Convertible

1969 Chevrolet Camaro Sport Coupe

1969 Chrysler 300 Two-Door Hardtop

1960 DeSoto Adventurer Two-Door Hardtop

1969 Mercury Cyclone CJ 428

CONSUMER GUIDE®